The Freedom of the Migrant

The Freedom of the Migrant

Objections to Nationalism

VILÉM FLUSSER

❦ ❦ ❦

Translated from the German by Kenneth Kronenberg

Edited and with an Introduction by Anke K. Finger

University of Illinois Press
Urbana, Chicago, and Springfield

The Freedom of the Migrant consists of English-language
translations of *Von der Freiheit des Migranten:
Einsprüche gegen den Nationalismus* and the essays
"Nomaden" and "Vom Fremden."

The Library of Congress cataloged the cloth edition as follows:
Flusser, Vilém, 1920–
[Von der Freiheit des Migranten. English]
The freedom of the migrant : objections to nationalism
/ Vilém Flusser ; translated from the German by
Kenneth Kronenberg ; edited and with an introduction
by Anke K. Finger.
p.   cm.
Includes bibliographical references.
ISBN 0-252-02817-1 (cloth : alk. paper)
1. Immigrants—Germany—Social conditions.
2. Immigrants—Civil rights—Germany. 3. Nationalism—
Germany. I. Finger, Anke K. II. Title.
JV8033F5813   2003
304.8′2—dc21   2002011802

PAPERBACK ISBN 978-0-252-07903-0

Contents

Acknowledgments

The selections in this book have been translated into English and edited with the permission of the copyright holder, Edith Flusser. Their original titles and sources are as follows:

The Challenge of the Migrant (Wohnung beziehen in der Heimatlosigkeit). Based on a paper presented in Weiler/Allgäu, August 1985. This German version is also available in *Bodenlos: Eine philosophische Autobiographie* (Fischer, 1999).

On the Alien (Vom Fremden). Published in *Jude Sein: Essays, Briefe, Fiktionen* (Philo Verlagsgesellschaft, 2000).

We Need a Philosophy of Emigration (Für eine Philosphie der Emigration). Presumably written in the seventies, unpublished.

To Be Unsettled, One First Has to Be Settled (Um entsetzt zu sein, muß man vorher sitzen). Published in *Basler Zeitung*, June 18, 1989. The manuscript is entitled "Vertreibung" (Expulsion).

Planning the Unplannable (Planung des Planlosen). Published in the *Frankfurter Allgemeine Zeitung*, August 6, 1970. The manuscript is entitled "Für eine Phänomenologie des Turismus."

From Guest to Guest Worker (Vom Gast zum Gastarbeiter). Undated manuscript.

Thinking about Nomadism (Nomadische Überlegungen). Published in *zeitmitschrift* 2 (1990).

Nomads (Nomaden). Published in Horst Gerhard Haberl, ed., *auf, und, davon: Eine Nomadologie der Neunziger* (Verlag Droschl, 1990).

Building Houses (Häuser bauen). Published in *Basler Zeitung*, March 22, 1989.

"How Goodly Are Your Tents, Jacob" ("Wie schön sind deine Zelte, Jakob"). Unpublished manuscript entitled "Zelte" (Tents).

Ex-perience (Er-fahrung). Published in *Perspektiven* 2 (1991).

Reunification or Networking? (Wiedervereinigung oder Vernetzung). Published in *Basler Zeitung*, April 10, 1990.

Does the French Nation Still Exist? (Gibt es die französische Nation noch immer?) Published in *Freitag*, November 15, 1991 and also available in *Nachgeschichte: Eine korrigierte Geschichtsschreibung* (Fischer, 1997).

Exile and Creativity (Exil und Kreativität). Published in *Spuren* 9 (Dec.–Jan. 1984–85).

Conversation between Vilém Flusser and Patrik Tschudin (Vilém Flusser im Gespräch mit Patrik Tschudin). Interview recorded on September 30, 1991. Broadcast (abbreviated version) on December 13, 1991 (Radio DRS-2, Switzerland).

The editor is grateful to Stephen Dowden, Richard J. Golsan, and Dominick LaCapra for their support of this project. The editor is particularly indebted to Kenneth Kronenberg for an always inspiring collaboration; to Andreas Ströhl for his advice and careful reading of the entire manuscript; to Douglas Brooks for his astute comments on the introduction; to the Center for Humanities Research at Texas A&M University for a grant to pursue research at the Flusser archive in Cologne; and to Silvia Wagnermaier, at the Cologne Academy of Media Arts, for her assistance with the archive. Special thanks go to Edith Flusser for her assistance, hospitality, and kindness; to Victoria Rosner and to Laura Frost for their generous help; and to Gregory Lewis for his encouragement and unfailing companionship. Finally, thanks to Benedict Anderson and the participants of his seminar on "late nationalism" at the 1999 School of Criticism and Theory (Cornell University) for stimulating debates on nationalism.

Introduction:
Vilém Flusser as Philosopher, Author, and Migrant

Anke K. Finger

Vilém Flusser's life and work embody the turmoil of the twentieth century. A refugee, an exile, and a migrant in various stages of his life, he transformed his mind, his hopes and memories, and his family and friends into places of constancy during an often complex and redundant set of personal and professional changes, some of them involuntary. Kept from finishing his university studies, he was dedicated throughout his life to the expansion of his and others' knowledge, to the study of language and communication, to the history of ideas—primarily in traditional European fashion—and to what one might call proximity theory, which deals with the fluctuating chances for dialogue and exchange in a world defined by the tangles of globalization, technology, and cultural difference. As such, Vilém Flusser can be best portrayed as an intellectual nomad who set up tent in innumerable "locales" of philosophical and historical thought. He was a passionate participant in debates and an inspired speaker, and he inspired, puzzled, irritated, and sometimes even exasperated his audiences.

Flusser was a prolific author whose topics range from the close observation of individual human habits in *Gesten* (Gestures, 1991) to the change in communicative codes over several thousands of years in *Die Schrift* (On writing, 1987). His writing style bespeaks his nomadic approach to learning, for he leaves few traces of the texts that lay the groundwork of his own ideas. This style makes for smooth and deceptively simple—to some even misleading—reading. The reader, intrigued and taken by Flusser's essayistic style, expectantly follows along the author's path but may stumble over some rough terrain in the reasoning. Yet most readers will feel that they have encountered the arguments of a deeply original and unorthodox thinker. Flusser's work triggers new ideas, questions, debate, criticism, and exchange—precisely what he aimed for in all his intellectual endeavors. Over the past several years, his ideas have increasingly attracted attention, particularly in Western Europe. Despite this growing fame and even cult status, Vilém Flusser remains an enigmatic figure. At least one source of the enigma is Flusser's personal background and development, both complicated by the range of his international influences and his intellectual nonconformity. According to Elizabeth Neswald, one of the few scholars who have written monographs on Flusser, these factors render his texts frequently as chimerical as they are analytical, and part of their fascination springs from the tension he builds into his construction of both the real and the projected worlds.[1]

The complexity that greets the new reader of Flusser's work may well be an outcome of the arguably incongruent Flussers known to his various past readerships. As a writer and lecturer who was compelled to develop great linguistic and cultural adaptability, he produced texts written in a multitude of languages, including Portuguese, German, French, and English.[2] Indeed, he is known in Brazil for a set of writings quite different from those that have appeared in Germany. His first book, *Lingua e Realidade* (1963), is available only in Portuguese, although it lays out the beginnings of his discussion on the "subject" and provides the groundwork for one of his central themes, language. Time will tell how well these different Flussers correlate to one another, and the development of international and critical response to the entirety of his thought will ultimately depend on the availability of translations. It is at this juncture that *The Freedom of the Migrant* contributes to the Anglo-American reception of Flusser's works.

On Flusser and His Concepts

Vilém Flusser was born in Prague on May 12, 1920, into an affluent Jewish family. His father was a professor of mathematics at Charles University, and Flusser had just embarked on his study of philosophy when he was forced to escape the Nazis in 1940. His father was killed in Buchenwald; his mother and sister were killed in Auschwitz. He was able to immigrate to Brazil via England with the family of his future wife, Edith Barth. In Brazil he studied philosophy privately while working in industry: "That meant that, during the day, one conducted business and at night one was able to philosophize."[3] In the early sixties a suddenly acquired reputation as a brilliant columnist led to teaching jobs at the University of São Paolo. Various positions as professor of philosophy of communication and of philosophy of science soon followed. During 1966–67 the Brazil State Department for Cultural Exchange sent him abroad to give lectures about Brazilian philosophers and their work. Later he began to build an international career with numerous guest lectures as a visiting professor at Berlin and other universities. After settling in France in 1975, he became better known in Europe and slowly rose to both academic and popular fame as a media phenomenologist and cultural critic. Beginning in 1975 he taught at the École d'Art d'Aix-en-Provence, the École Nationale de la Photographie Arles, and at the Université de Provence Aix-Marseille. His last appointment was with the Ruhr-Universität Bochum in Germany. On November 27, 1991, he died from injuries sustained in an automobile accident outside Prague.

As a media theorist Vilém Flusser examined what he found to be substantial changes in our epistemology, particularly changes that are emerging as globalized circulatory networks and increasingly visual stimulation challenge our linear and literary learning. For Flusser, these new approaches to understanding different cultures and customs both inside and outside individual topographies will radically alter intracultural relations in the future. Accordingly Flusser argues that contemporary societies are in flux and need to learn how to switch from the literary to the visual, from the national to the global.

These are popular ideas among Flusser's readers in Germany, where his ideas and texts have thrived over the last two decades and where most of his writing has been published. Furthermore, despite his former status as a cultural attaché assigned to propagate Brazilian philosophy, his inclusion in a volume discussing contemporaries such as

Hans Blumenberg, Hans-Georg Gadamer, Jürgen Habermas, Hans Jonas, Niklas Luhmann, and Carl Friedrich von Weizsäcker suggests that he is now considered a German philosopher, at least in Germany.[4] In this context, it is certainly noteworthy that Flusser probably thought of himself more as an author than a philosopher or media theorist. In one of Flusser's last interviews, conducted by Daniela Kloock in October 1991, she inquired, in reference to Nietzsche, whether he would deem himself a "gay scientist": "I would not call myself a philosopher," replied Flusser. "I think about things that happen all around me. My memory is host to a collection of information that helps me to store and specify my own information; I then type the product into my typewriter . . . and the result is a text."[5] No doubt this is something of a simplistic assessment of his efforts, but Flusser's answer is consistent with his concept of the telematic society and his principle of dialogue or theory of proximity. Elsewhere he has referred to this kind of work as the work of the author: "What does an author do? He collects information—located in works already produced—according to the criteria of his time and culture. To this collection of information he adds more information which he has gained in his own life. . . . He *processes* this accumulated amount of information, that is, it is being diversified and computed in order to form new information."[6]

Whether we define Flusser as a philosopher or an author, the activities he describes point to the overarching principle of his theories and concepts, namely, the principle of dialogue. While his reception in Germany is still primarily based on his reputation as a media philosopher, some scholars are beginning to place more emphasis on his significance as a cultural philosopher or critic. Ingeborg Breuer, Peter Leusch, and Dieter Mersch, for example, point to the ethical and historical implications of Flusser's theories of communication.[7] More significantly, Andreas Ströhl stresses that "Flusser is . . . a media theorist only because it necessitates the application of his theory of communication—derived from his fundamental distinction between dialogue and discourse—to the current situation of our society."[8] This distinction defines dialogue as that which produces information and discourse as that which collects information. Ideally the two coincide and interconnect, so that to live in a telematically networked society is to be both recipient and sender at once, ever processing and ever producing.

What is the "telematic society," one of Flusser's pivotal concepts derived from the hope for dialogue? Forced into obligatory "private study," that is, the life of an autodidact, by personal and historical circumstances, Flusser developed his own eclectic knowledge and collected a resourceful international group of colleagues and friends, among them writers, artists, journalists, and professors. The "privacy" of his studies arguably produced a gigantic imaginary network of interaction and ideas that allowed Flusser to be lifted out of his individual and perhaps solitary intellectual context. Accordingly, he refers to the telematic society in the essay "Ex-perience" in the following way:

> Let us imagine that our central nervous system were to extend around the globe like a net. Let us further imagine that it would constitute something like a *neurosphere* situated between the biosphere and the atmosphere. What I am suggesting is not science fiction but the model on which the telematic society now being built is based. What we need to do is imagine such a neurosphere as a network of human nerves as well as material and nonmaterial cables. And we must further imagine human brains and artificial intelligences at the nodal intersections of such a network. Such a neurosphere spanning the globe would function to compute into experience all stimuli incessantly streaming in from all directions and to transform these experiences into decisions and actions. Seen this way, the telematic society would be a mechanism for experience, a global machine for the realization of potentials.

Yet Flusser is talking here not about the worldwide network of gateways and fiber-optic cables but rather about ancient Judeo-Christian ideas. In particular, Flusser's thought builds on what Martin Buber has established as the juxtaposition of "I" and "thou," as the "meeting" that is not a "we" but the mutual recognition of one in the other.[9] Certainly the digital revolution of the 1990s has triggered a version of such a dialogue, foregrounding the *tele-* in human communication, bringing us closer via networks. However, as Flusser often claimed, discourse, the collecting and storing of information, is part of this process of dialoguing and poses as the threatening "we" should the relationship not be kept in balance. A "cybernetic democracy," as his concept has been called elsewhere, would consequently be in danger. Not surprisingly, in the context of this edition, dialogue and discourse face off as a juxtaposition of the world as both a global village and a compound of nationalisms. Since Flusser ably merges memory and experience in this regard, the texts he produced offer a plethora of points for discussion.

Essentially Vilém Flusser envisioned an exchange of information that leads to a synthesis, that is, to understanding and meaning, capable of bringing people and cultures closer. Apart from arguing for a telematic society and, ultimately, for a renewed engagement with dialogue based on Buber's philosophy, he was also invested in a theory of proximity contained in his notion of telematic society. In an interview conducted by Thomas Mießgang on March 13, 1991, Flusser explained that "at the moment a science of closeness is emerging, the so-called study of proximity [Proxemik]. And if I consider closeness a fundamental term, if I say: something is close by, then I have abolished the difference between space and time. 'Close by' implies a tangible distance both in terms of time and space and it also contains a 'bringing closer.' This is a Judeo-Christian principle. The love of your neighbor thus becomes possible. Love of your neighbor instead of humanism— that is an important aspect of the word *telematics*."[10] For the context of the essays included in this edition, Flusser's theory of proximity or closeness acquires particular validity as he examines the "technicalities" or machines—television, computers, means of transportation, dwellings—of dialogue not by the way they bring us into the world but by the extent to which the world enters our homes. In "To Be Unsettled, One First Has to Be Settled," Flusser suggests, for example, that "the expellees whom we occasionally see on television show us that to which we would do well to aspire." How so? According to Flusser, refugees, migrants, expellees, and nomads by definition live unsettled lives, and they may deem their existence either one of self-determination or one of suffering. These unsettled lives reflect back on us, however, and force us to examine our settledness—hence Flusser's request for a "creative house," a "node in the network of interpersonal relations," perforated by cables that work both ways, like the telephone and not like television. In fact, Flusser encourages us to "exorcise" our "seatedness in habit" to realize how much we are just like the expellees or migrants who stream into our houses: lodged in "unreality" that we can escape only if we answer to the "call" of the other.

In the longest and possibly most significant essay of this collection, Flusser illustrates the simultaneity of suffering and bliss a migrant, expellee, refugee, or exile can experience if he or she analyzes the potential in this externalized position:

> Homeland is not an eternal value but rather a function of a specific technology; still, whoever loses it suffers. This is because we are attached to heimat by many bonds, most of which are hidden and not accessible to consciousness. Whenever these attachments tear or are torn asunder, the individual experiences this painfully, almost as a surgical invasion of his most intimate person. When I was forced to leave Prague (or got up the courage to flee), I felt that the universe was crumbling. I fell into the error of confusing my private self with the outside world. It was only after I realized, painfully, that these now severed attachments had bound me that I was overcome by that strange dizziness of liberation and freedom which everywhere characterizes the free spirit. . . . The transformation of the question "Free from what?" to "Free for what?"—an inversion that is characteristic of freedom gained—has since accompanied me like a basso continuo on my migrations. All we nomads who have emerged from it share in the collapse of settledness.

Nomad, migrant, heimat, and exile are notions that Flusser interweaves with his principle of dialogue. Over the last decades, and specifically since the establishment of Benedict Anderson's paradigm of "imagined community," the parameters of the historical nation-state and definitions of citizenship generated in part by the exponential growth of ever more hybrid communities and identities have come under scrutiny.[11]

The translation of Flusser's work is now timely because migration, nationalism, and ethnic identity, in combination with global communication and digitalization, are becoming ever more connected in the economic realm as well as in academic areas of research. Indeed, Flusser was among the first writers to recognize the need to examine their interconnections. Furthermore, in view of his principle of dialogue, the development of his ideas exemplifies the rapid changes cultures have undergone over the course of the last decades; these changes require close examination if the cultures are to engage in any meaningful form of interchange. That Flusser himself frequently operated as the "token" migrant and ethnic minority adds to the importance of his critical observations.

Appropriately, an analysis of his writings suggests that he located the origin of his ideas within the theoretical parameters of several comparable thinkers and—with exceptions—fellow migrants. Hannah Arendt, Walter Benjamin, Edmund Husserl, Martin Buber, and Ludwig Wittgenstein influenced his investigations of phenomenology, (Jewish) history, and language. Flusser's American influences, inspirations, and contacts included Noam Chomsky, Sidney Hook, Arthur Kroker, and Giorgio de Santillana. In this volume Wittgenstein, Hegel, Nietzsche, and others provide the foundation for a discussion of the subject-object relation in general and of the perforation of our houses and lives that enables the proximity of the other in particular.

Despite his international career, Flusser's works did not receive much attention until the 1980s, when he published his book on photography, a text that makes plain his engagement with phenomenological models in examining "images" in culture and the digital revolution. Over the years he has gained further recognition in Germany, France, the United States, and parts of Eastern Europe. His publications reflect this reception. So far, two German publishers have undertaken editions of his writings: European Photography has brought out a ten-volume edition of Flusser's important texts from the 1980s on television, photography, writing, and the future of images. The Bollmann Verlag's five-volume edition (fourteen volumes were anticipated) is now published in paperback under the auspices of the wellknown S. Fischer Verlag and aims to encompass the entirety of his philosophical and critical writings, including the work on emigration and exile, Jewish religion and culture, and history. Recently, the Philo-Verlag has reissued several texts that were long out of print. Currently no one publisher is publishing Flusser's texts, and his current and potential readers will have to wait until a complete critical edition becomes available in any language.

Flusser in the Anglo-American Context

Vilém Flusser's first profound encounter with the Anglo-American world occurred during the short time he spent in England after he escaped Prague and before he left for Brazil. Struggling with the absurdities of human existence in a time of war and persecution, Flusser reports in his autobiographical *Bodenlos* (1992) an increasing indifference toward the warring parties as well as the values they represented: everything becomes leveled; everything possesses either the same or no validity. "The result of this indifference," Flusser continues, "was my opening up to new horizons. English culture, English philosophy, English being-in-the-world,[12] and the English language, in particular, became unclosed. And with it America with its inexhaustible treasures. One began to look back on Prague with astonishment. This narrow world of tight angles couldn't possibly compare to Anglo-Saxon spaces. How could it ever have been considered the center? But the path to the English world was merely a transit to completely different views—to the realization that narrowness constitutes not a geographical but an existential condition."[13] Narrowness of disposition, of thought, and of interests continued to be at the forefront of that against which Flusser argued for decades to come. Unfortunately, as the following correspondence suggests, narrowness often translates into institutional procedures. As such, Flusser was occasionally penalized for never having completed a formal education or receiving a degree.

On November 2, 1962, Flusser, a recent appointee for philosophy of science at the University of São Paulo, posted the following letter of inquiry to Professor Lionel Ruby at the American Philosophical Association, requesting information on the prospect of teaching in the American university system:

> [Brazil] is at once stimulating and frustrating for one interested in philosophical study and investigation. It is stimulating, because practically anything one does is pioneer work. . . . It is frustrating, because "official" intellectual groups . . . are rigidly divided in two rival camps, the Marxist and the Catholic. . . . This is the reason why I feel I need the experience of intimate contact with a radically different spiritual atmosphere. . . . My

frustration is a social one. I am unable to submit to the prevailing spirit at the State and the Pontifical Faculties. I feel that my work would be both more fertile and more effective in the independent atmosphere of a University in the United States. Mr. Delmez tells me that your institutions are "extremely degree conscious." I hold no degree, having left my home, Prague, when it was occupied by the Nazis, at the age of twenty. My studies have, therefore, been private. Do you believe that there is a possibility of my working in one of your Universities in the sense outlined above, inspite of this? What I want is contact with your intellectuals, and the possibility to teach, write, and publish. . . . I should add that I speak several languages (Portuguese, English, Czech, German, French, etc.) but that my philosophical back-ground is mostly German and English. The works that influenced me most are "Principia Mathematica," "Tractatus Logico-Philosophicus," "Sein und Zeit" and the "Nietzsche" of Heidegger.

Forty years ago the degree consciousness of the American academy was of course no more lax than it is today. Accordingly, on December 18, 1962, the chairman of the Committee on Information Service: Vacancies and Personnel responded, "It would be extremely difficult for you to get a teaching position without a degree." He suggested that Flusser first seek "some kind of connection with the University of San Paulo [sic] so that [he] could have some kind of academic status." He should then write to the leading departments of philosophy to obtain a graduate fellowship, complete with stipend and the option of an assistantship "involving some teaching." A month later Flusser replied:

I have been appointed "effective fellow" of the Instituto Brasileiro de Filosofia on December 20, 1962, which, in this country, is the official academic institution for philosophical activities. . . . I cannot, however, hope for a "cátedra" . . . since none is vacant or will be in the next future. On the other hand, I cannot apply for a doctor's degree, because, according to Brazilian laws, I would have to pass first through primary and secondary schools, since my certificates of "maturity" and six semesters at the Prague University are not recognized. On the other hand, a doctor's degree is no use here to me, since I am fairly well known through my publications and have been offered teaching appointments . . . repeatedly. Would my membership at the "Instituto" be considered "academic status" in your country?[14]

Predictably, no American position or academic connection materialized from this exchange, and we know only that Flusser later presented occasional talks at several American universities, including MIT and Columbia University. I cite these letters at length because they suggest some of the challenges facing a migrant philosopher and author for reasons that are endemic to the essays collected in this volume.

Today some of Flusser's work has found resonance with English-speaking readers interested in the "digital thinker," especially a few English-language publications that examine globalization from the perspectives of media theory and art. Nonetheless, only a handful of his publications that investigate globalization from the perspectives of media theory and art have been made available. With the exception of Flusser's book on photography, *Toward a Philosophy of Photography* (1984), available in numerous languages, and *The Shape of Things: A Philosophy of Design* (1999), few of Flusser's major writings have been translated into English. Occasional and often abbreviated essays are available in scattered magazines—for example, *Design-Issues, Main Currents,* and *Leonardo*—and in books such as Timothy Druckrey's *Electronic Culture* (1995) and Joachimides and Rosenthal's *Metropolis* (1991). In addition, during the late 1980s and early 1990s, Flusser infrequently wrote short columns for New York's *Artforum International.* In two journals, *Yale Journal of Criticism* (6, no. 2 [1993]) and a special issue of *Weber Studies* devoted to science, technology, and the arts (14, no. 1 [1997]), Elizabeth Wilson and Andreas Ströhl, respectively, have provided the only general English-language introductions to Flusser's work with a short summary of his major texts. These texts include *Die Schrift* (Writing [1987], a brief history of the alphanumeric code and the possibilities inherent to its successive codes), *Angenommen* (Supposed [1989], on futuristic models of society), *Gesten* (Gestures [1991], a phenomenological investigation of everyday actions such as writing, smoking, and using one's hands), *Nachgeschichte* (Posthistory [1991], a contribution to the debate on the end of history and future social constellations), and *Bodenlos* (Rootless [1992], a philosophical autobiography). The list does not include *Vom Subjekt zum Projekt* (From subject to project [1998]), *Lob der Oberflächlichkeit* (In praise of superficiality [1993]), *Kommunikologie* (Communicology [1998]), *Jude Sein*

(Being Jewish [1995]), and others. In short, easily accessible information on Flusser in the English-speaking world is scarce. The first English-language anthology of Flusser's writings, edited by Andreas Ströhl, slightly improves this situation.[15]

Nonetheless, the previously mentioned translated texts offer only a very incomplete picture of Flusser's thought on the current transformation of communities and nations. The Flusser represented in this collection of essays offers important, wide-ranging, and unique perspectives on communication, nomadism, housing, nationalism, migrant cultures, and Jewish identity. Many readers who work in a number of areas related to cultural studies and communication will find in Flusser's work a new source of ideas about contemporary culture. Indeed, his intriguing and original commentaries on human behavior and its practical and theoretical implications challenge us to generate new critical discourses with which we can locate the origins and agents of cultural change and dialogue. As such, Flusser's work is primarily philosophical and essayistic in the best sense of these terms, and he is a worthy participant in the currently vivid and prolific debates on nationalism, migrant culture, and ethnic identity in various fields.

Notes

1. Elizabeth Neswald, *Medien-Theologie: Das Werk Vilém Flussers* (Cologne: Böhlau, 1998). For a more recent analysis of Flusser's work see Rainer Guldin, *Philosophieren zwischen den Sprachen: Vilém Flussers Phänomenologie der Bodenlosigkeit* (Berlin: Philo-Verlag, 2002); and Gustavo Bernardo Krause, *A duvida de Flusser* (Rio de Janeiro: Editora Globo, 2002).

2. For an exhaustive list of Flusser's publications in various languages, see Klaus Sander, *Flusser-Quellen: Eine kommentierte Bibliographie Vilém Flussers von 1960–2000* (Göttingen: European Photography, 2002).

3. Quoted in "Utopie der telematischen Gesellschaft: Zur Medien- und Kulturphilosophie Vilém Flussers," in Ingeborg Breuer, Peter Leusch, and Dieter Mersch, *Welten im Kopf: Profile der Gegenwartsphilosophie* (Hamburg: Rotbuch, 1996), 82. My translation.

4. Ibid.

5. Daniela Kloock, *Von der Schrift- zur Bild(schirm)kultur: Analyse aktueller Medientheorien* (Berlin: Volker Spiess, 1995), 200. My translation.

6. Vilém Flusser, "Vom Autor oder vom Wachsen," in *Kunst Machen? Gespräche und Essays,* ed. Florian Rötzer and Sara Rogenhofer (Munich: Karl Boer, 1991), 68. My translation.

7. Breuer, Leusch, and Mersch, "Utopie," 82.

8. Andreas Ströhl, "Flusser und der Dialog: Negentropische Klimmzüge über der Bodenlosigkeit," unpublished manuscript, Flusser archive, Kunsthochschule für Medien, Cologne, 9.

9. Martin Buber, *Ich und Du* (Gütersloh: Gütersloher Verlag, 1997 [1923]). For a short discussion, see Emmanuel Levinas, *Outside the Subject,* trans. Michael B. Smith (Stanford, Calif.: Stanford University Press, 1994), 4–48.

10. Thomas Mießgang, *X-Sample: Gespräche am Rande der Zeit* (Vienna: Passagen Verlag, 1993), 26.

11. Benedict Anderson, *Imagined Communities: Reflections on the Origin and Spread of Nationalism* (London: Verso, 1983).

12. German: das englische In-der-Welt-sein.

13. Vilém Flusser, *Bodenlos* (Bensheim: Bollmann Verlag, 1992), 36. My translation.

14. Correspondence in English, typescript, Flusser archive.

15. Andreas Ströhl, ed., *Flusser: Writings* (Minneapolis: University of Minnesota Press, 2002).

Editor's Note

This edition is a translation of the German original, entitled *Von der Freiheit des Migranten: Einsprüche gegen den Nationalismus,* first published in 1994 and edited and arranged posthumously by Stefan Bollmann. Three of the essays included in the original have been replaced by the English translations of "Nomaden" (Nomads) and "Vom Fremden" (On the Alien). Footnotes on pp. 3 and 105 are translations of footnotes added by Stefan Bollmann in the German original. Flusser's use of the German language is inspired by his attention to etymology and wordplay. Any translation is necessarily a compromise between the two languages involved. This is even more the case with Flusser, who places great emphasis on the multitudinous connotations of key words. As most of Flusser's writings on language and linguistics still await review and commentary, however, this collection simply provides the German original for a few elusive terms without speculating about their significance in Flusser's writing.

The Freedom of the Migrant

❦ ❦ ❦ The Challenge of the Migrant*

Although it goes against my usual practice and steers us away from the subject of heimat and its loss, I would nonetheless like to tell the reader about my own loss of heimat.[†] I was born in Prague, and my ancestors appear to have lived in the Golden City for more than a thousand years. I am a Jew, and the adage "Next year in Jerusalem" accompanied me through childhood. For decades now I have taken part in the attempt to synthesize a Brazilian culture out of a mixture of Western and Eastern European, African, East Asian, and Indian cultural elements. I now live in a village in Provence, and I have become assimilated into the weft and warp of this timeless place. I was brought up in the German

---

*German title: "Wohnung beziehen in der Heimatlosigkeit," literally "Taking residence in homelessness."

[†]The English *home* does not fully encompass the German *Heimat,* which allows for connotations such as home, homeland, and region (of one's origins), often accompanied by notions of nostalgia, even myth; *Heimat* itself contains *Heim,* referring to one's family home or "[being] at home." To some in postwar Germany, *Heimat* is still reminiscent of the Nazis' ideological fixation on home and homeland and the appropriation of territory, making the term potentially a synonym of "Blut und Boden" and thus suspicious for casual use even today. On the other hand, in the seventies and eighties the term regained currency in connection with the notorious *"Historikerstreit,"* the *"Ostpolitik"* of Chancellor Willy Brandt, and the popular TV series "Heimat" by Edgar Reitz. As Elizabeth Boa and Rachel Palfreyman summarize: "The sheer persistence of the concept of Heimat through the twists and turns of German history suggests that it may connote a deep-seated psychological need, which may even be intrinsic to identity formation, but which is mediated differently through changing history and in different cultural contexts. The term has many different usages in the fields of law, politics, the natural sciences, anthropology, sociology, psychology, philosophy, religion, and literature as well as in political discourse" (Elizabeth Boa and Rachel Palfreyman, eds., *Heimat—A German Dream: Regional Loyalties and National Identity in German Culture, 1890–1990* [Oxford: Oxford University Press, 2000], 23). For these reasons, the English translation retains the German original. For an extensive discussion of heimat, including the most recent literature, see Peter Blickle, *Heimat: A Critical Theory of the German Idea of Homeland* (Rochester, N.Y.: Camden House, 2002).

culture, and I have reconnected with it over the past several years. In short, I am now without heimat because too many heimats reside within me. This manifests itself daily in my work. I feel at home in at least four languages, and I feel challenged and even forced to translate and then back-translate everything that I write.

What makes matters more difficult, but also inspires me, is that I am interested in the phenomenon of communication between people, that is, in the gaps between points of view and the structures that serve to bridge them. In all probability this interest derives from my own un-settledness. It allows and even forces me to experience and work through what is transcendent about heimats but also to theorize about them. The following essay documents my concrete experience, daily processing, and theoretical consideration of the subject of heimat and homelessness.

First, I want to draw a sharp distinction between *Heimat* and *Wohnung* [home]. In so doing, I am painfully aware of having to play with the German language. In the languages with which I am familiar, only the Czech word *domov* is equivalent to the German *Heimat,* and this probably thanks to the pressure German exerted on Czech over the past several hundred years. It may perhaps be that the concept of *Heimat* is native only to German—the concept, perhaps, but what about the experience? I have my doubts even about the experience. Does the farmer in Robion, Provence, experience his historically mul-tilayered and many-storied heimat (on which late Paleolithic, Neo-lithic, Ligurian, Greek, Roman, Visigoth, Burgundian, Arab, Frankish, Provençal, Italian, and French ancestors all labored) in the same way as the migrant Brazilian farmworker sees his *terra* or the Israeli kib-butznik his *Eretz Israel*?

Although humans are settlers and have been dwellers for much of our history, we have lacked heimat. Now that evidence is beginning to accumulate that we are leaving 10,000 years of Neolithic settledness behind us, it is instructive to think about the relatively short time that we have been settled. The so-called values that we are in the process of giving up along with our settledness—including possessions, the second-class status of women, the division of labor, and heimat—are now shown to be less eternal values than functions of agriculture and cattle breeding. Our troubled emergence from agriculture and its industrial atavisms into the still-unmapped regions of postindustrial and posthistorical society (hinc sunt leones)* is facilitated by such considerations. In this image we, the countless millions of migrants (whether guest workers, exiles, refugees, or intellectuals shuttling between one Granary Seminar† and the next) recognize ourselves not as outsiders but as vanguards of the future. The Vietnamese in California, the Turks in Germany, the Palestinians in the Gulf states, and Russian scientists at Harvard—they are no longer pitiable victims whom we need help to regain their lost heimats but rather models whom we should emulate, if we have the requisite courage. Of course, such thoughts are appropriate only in the minds of expellees, the migrants, not in those of the expellers, those who remain behind. Because migration, although a creative activity, also entails suffering, just as action often originates in suffering ("Who never ate with tears his bread . . .").

⚜ ⚜ ⚜   Homeland is not an eternal value but rather a function of a specific technology; still, whoever loses it suffers. This is because we are attached to heimat by many bonds, most of which are hidden and not accessible to consciousness. Whenever these attachments tear or are torn asunder, the individual experiences this painfully, almost as a surgical invasion of his most intimate person. When I was forced to leave Prague (or got up the courage to flee), I felt that the universe was crumbling. I fell into the error of confusing my private self with the outside world. It was only after I realized, painfully, that these now severed attachments had bound me that I was overcome by that strange dizziness of liberation and freedom which everywhere characterizes the free spirit. I first experienced this sense of freedom in London, in that country that strikes many Continentals as almost Chinese, at the beginning of the war, during a time of foreboding about the coming human horror in the camps. The transformation of the question "Free

*Latin: "next [from here on] there are lions." Roman mapmakers used the term to indicate (potentially dangerous) terra incognita (I would like to thank Bruce Bethell for providing this information [AF]).

†This text is based on a talk given on the subject of homeland and its loss [Heimat und Heimatlosigkeit] at the second so-called Granary Seminar in Weiler (Allgäu).

from what?" to "Free for what?"—an inversion that is characteristic of freedom gained—has since accompanied me like a basso continuo on my migrations. All we nomads who have emerged from it share in the collapse of settledness.

The attachments that bind the settled person to the people and things of his heimat are mostly hidden. They extend beyond adult consciousness into childish, infantile, and probably even fetal and transpersonal regions, into memory that is not well articulated, barely articulated, or completely unarticulated. A mundane example: the Czech dish called *svickova* [beef tenderloin roast] awakens in me feelings that are hard to analyze but to which the German word *Heimweh* [homesickness] comes close. The loss of heimat allows fresh air into this hidden feeling, this comfortable murkiness, and shows it for what it is: the seat of most (perhaps even all) prejudice, that is, judgments that are made prior to all conscious judgments.

The feeling for heimat, so celebrated in prose and poetry, this mysterious rootedness in infantile, fetal, and transpersonal regions of the psyche, cannot withstand the sober analysis that he who is without heimat is both duty bound and able to undertake. It is true that just after he leaves his heimat and begins to undertake this analysis, the feeling for heimat will grab hold of his guts and make him feel as if they were being turned inside out. The German word *Heimweh* and the French *nostalgie* capture this less well than does the Portuguese *saudade*. But after the transformation of expulsion into the dizziness of freedom and the inversion of the question "Free from what?" into "Free for what?" alluded to earlier, the mysterious rootedness comes to be seen as obscurantist enmeshment that must be cut through like a Gordian knot. Only then does the person analyzing himself recognize the degree to which this mysterious rootedness in heimat has clouded his ability to see reality clearly. He then realizes not only that each heimat blinds in its own particular way those who are enmeshed in it, and that all heimats are equal in this sense, but also that clear judgment, decision making, and action become possible only after one sees oneself clear of this enmeshment. In my own case, after cutting through one Gordian knot after another—of Prague, London, São Paulo—not only have I become convinced of the equivalence of all prejudices native to those places, as well as of those native to Robion; I have also recognized that my freedom to judge, decide, and act becomes greater each time I sever a knot. This recognition enables me to cut through knots with ever-increasing virtuosity. My forced emigration from Prague was a terrible experience; leaving Robion would probably be no more than a decision freely taken, entailing getting in the car and driving off. This is why Zionism exerts no existential pull on me, despite my sympathies.

⚜ ⚜ ⚜   The mysterious feeling of heimat attaches to people and things. Both are bathed in this mystery. I do not think that it is necessary to talk here about the perniciousness of being enthralled by things. Not only do objects that are made sacred engender conditionality (that is, they limit freedom), but they are personalized as well (because one comes to love them). This confusion of things with persons, which is an ontological error, mistaking an "it" for a "you," is precisely what the prophets referred to as heathenism, and it is the magical thinking that philosophers have tried to overcome. However, our mysterious bonds to human beings deserve consideration because they pose the fundamental problem of freedom.

In this regard I have had two contradictory experiences. All the people in Prague with whom I had a mysterious bond were murdered. All of them. The Jews in gas chambers, the Czechs in the Resistance, the Germans at the Russian Front. All the people in São Paulo with whom I have a mysterious bond are still alive, and I am still in contact with them. Paradoxically, this made slicing through the Prague Gordian knot easier than doing so to the one associated with São Paulo, even though the mystery that tied me to the former was deeper and darker than that which tied me to the latter. Indeed, a macabre experience.

The mysterious bonds that bind one to the people of one's heimat (such as love and friendship, but also hate and enmity) pull at the emigrant because they place in question the freedom that he has gained through his suffering. They represent the dialogical bonds of responsibility for, and defense of, others. Is the freedom of the migrant merely an irresponsible, solipsistic freedom that bobs about over many places, never settling? Has he simply gained his freedom at the cost of being with others? Or is aloneness without responsibility the fate of the migrant, as romantic poets would have it? The transformation from expulsion into freedom that I talked about previously answers this question in the negative. I was thrown into my first heimat at birth without being asked. The bonds that tied me to others were largely imposed on me. In the freedom that I have now achieved, I myself weave my connections with others, and I do this in concert with them. The responsibility that I have for others has not been forced on me; it is something that I have taken on myself. Unlike those who remained behind, I am not mysteriously enmeshed with others but have freely chosen my relationships. These relationships are not less emotional or sentimental than those enmeshments, but they are more freely entered into.

I believe that this elucidates the meaning of being free. It has nothing to do with cutting one's attachments to others; instead, it concerns weaving relationships in concert with them. The migrant becomes free not when he denies his lost heimat but rather when he holds it in memory. I am a citizen of Prague, of São Paulo, and of Robion, and I am a Jew and at home within German culture. I deny none of this; rather, I underscore it to negate it.

⚜ ⚜ ⚜   Sociologists would like us to believe that foreigners (such as sociologists or persons without a heimat) can learn the secret codes of heimat, because after all, the natives had to learn them too, which confirms the meaning of initiation rites among so-called primitive peoples. A person without heimat should therefore be able to wander from one heimat to another and settle in each one, if only he carries with him all the necessary keys needed to unlock them. But the reality is very different. The secret codes are not, in general, conscious rules but rather are spun largely from unconscious habits. What is characteristic of habits is that one is not conscious of them. To be able to settle in a new heimat, an immigrant must first learn the secret code consciously—and then forget it again. If the code becomes conscious, then its rules are exposed as something banal and not sacred. For the native who is settled, the immigrant is even more alien and strange than the migrant outside his door because he exposes as banal what the native considers sacred. He is worthy of hatred and he is detestable because he reveals the heimat's beauty as prettified kitsch. A polemical dialogue develops between the beautiful native and the detestable immigrant, which can end either in pogrom, a change in the heimat, or the native's liberation from his own attachments. My own experience in Brazil provides an example.

❧ ❧ ❧   First, I would like to free the concept "Brazil" from the Eurocentric prejudices with which it is encrusted (Third World, underdevelopment, exploitation, etc.). Of course, prejudices—that is, judgments that form preconsciously—are native to all heimats. Until the middle of the nineteenth century the population of Brazil consisted of three social strata. One stratum consisted of the Portuguese, some of whom had fled their heimat and some of whom administered the country for Portugal. Then there were Africans, who were brought there as slaves. And the country was populated by indigenous Indians, who were increasingly pushed into the hinterland (these indigenous Indians were themselves divided into the former rulers, the Tupis, and a lower, subject caste, known contemptuously as Tupinambas). During the second half of the nineteenth century, when slavery was abolished and unemployed Africans began to flock to the cities, a call was put out for European immigrants, initially from northern Italy, to work in agriculture (coffee, cotton, sugarcane). The first wave of immigration was followed by immigration from Poland, Syria and Lebanon, Japan, and additional waves from Portugal. When I arrived, Jews formed the most recent wave, but others followed, until immigration dwindled and then dried up in the 1960s. It is important to remember that this immigration mainly affected the South of the country, while leaving the North virtually untouched, which meant that Brazil was divided into two regions. At present there is a massive movement of people from the Northeast into the South, and the images that Europeans see on television are largely of this massive migration.

Although there was constant talk of a Brazilian heimat in poetry and prose before the liberation of the slaves, the reality (the notorious *realidade brasileira*) put the lie to this talk. The Portuguese rulers, who were concentrated in the port cities, anxiously awaited the latest news from their old heimats, from Lisbon and Paris. They felt expelled.

Africans constituted the largest portion of the population, but they had no conscious relationship with Africa. The human beings who were disgorged naked from slave ships on the Brazilian shore possessed in their inner selves, numbed by hard work, only the memory of the patterns of their lost culture. These manifested themselves in music, dance, and religious rites, forming the foundations of any future Brazilian heimat. The indigenous Indians, who were pushed ever further into the forests, were never included as genuine Brazilians: they were relegated to the background, sometimes celebrated as mythic objects, occasionally brutally raped. Brazil (and Argentina and Uruguay) differs from the rest of Latin America in that the indigenous Indians merely form an ideologically veiled background there.

Since the end of the nineteenth century, European, Middle Eastern, and Asian immigrants have attempted to come to terms with Brazil as a heimat. But is it even possible for such heterogeneous elements to weave the sorts of mysterious attachments that they had known in their old heimats? The Portuguese language was a starting point. In comparison to the language spoken in Portugal, it was both archaic (harboring elements from the Renaissance) and feral (with African inclusions). But this is precisely what allowed Portuguese to serve as a lingua franca between, say, Arabic and Japanese settlers. Would it be possible to create a Brazilian language that was capable of both bearing and transmitting [*tragen und übertragen*] a Brazilian culture that could then serve to transform the territory of Brazil into a heimat for a future society? To my mind this question, which so engaged the people involved, formed the substrate in which everything that has since been elaborated in this century—from Brasilia to the bossa nova—was rooted.

When I arrived in Brazil, I found myself caught up in this excitement the moment I was able to free myself somewhat from the gas chambers. I enthusiastically joined in the creation of a new, humane, and unprejudiced heimat. Only with the *golpe*, the coup d'état by the army, did disillusionment set in. And not because I saw it as a reactionary intervention, as had many European observers, but rather because I discerned in it the first actualization of a Brazilian heimat. I want to delve into my disillusionment with my Brazilian heimat (and all heimats by extension) at greater length.

When the waves of immigration began in the nineteenth century, Brazil was an existential no-man's land. It was nobody's heimat, and hence the battle cry of the patriots who wanted to bring about a heimat: *Este pais tem dono.** This was not like an African, Asian, or Andean colony in which colonists ruled natives; it was more like the United States, an empty land from which the natives were driven. This was why the immigrants were received not as detested foreigners but rather as comrades who shared the fate of being without heimat. (Because of a lack of time I cannot examine the differences between Brazil and the United States.) This reception, so lacking in prejudice, was so different from the experience of the European heimats from which they had been expelled that it would have appeared odious not to become engaged. In addition, everyone was a pioneer in this no-man's land. In my own case, a Brazilian philosophy still had to be elaborated in concert with other comrades who shared my fate. And so we began to spin out dialogical threads between ourselves, ones that we did not inherit at birth in our lost heimats, but ones that we freely produced. And with this I recognized what makes patriotism (both local and national) so disastrous: it hallows human attachments that have been imposed and in so doing neglects and prejudices the ones that we develop ourselves. It places family relationship above relationships of choice, what is genuinely or only ideologically biological above friendship and love. I was overcome by a dizzying feeling of freedom: now I was free to choose my neighbors.

As long as Brazilian society welcomed new waves of immigrants, this weaving of a secret code, of a future Brazilian heimat, this transformation of adventure into habit and this hallowing of habit, remained charged with excitement. The network being woven remained open. For example, the philosophical institute in which Italian students of Croce, German Heidegger scholars, Portuguese followers of Ortega, Jewish positivists from Eastern Europe, Belgian Catholics, and Anglo-Saxon pragmatists took part had to open itself up to Japanese students of Zen Buddhism, a Lebanese mystic, and a Chinese literary scholar, and it had to make room for a Talmudist from Western Europe as well.

---

*Portuguese: "This country has a master."

In spite of this, it began to become institutionalized. Admittance became increasingly more difficult, and prejudices started to crystallize. This was symptomatic of its very success in creating a new heimat.

Two phenomena of the 1950s also had to be taken into account. The first may be denoted by the term *defasagem;** the second, by *populismo.* To the extent to which an autonomous core Brazilianism began to be elaborated, vital contact with the more important centers (especially those in America) began to close off, and I recognized what I had given up by becoming actively engaged with Brazil—freedom from geographic attachment. I began to wonder whether, given the Information Revolution then taking place, all attachment to a geographical region was not in fact reactionary, whether one should give up the advantages of not having a heimat at all.

The second phenomenon—the more radical—was *populismo.* Socioeconomically, the great majority of the population lived a seminomadic existence during the 1950s, following the harvests in misery, hunger, and disease. The great challenge was to create a heimat out of this cultureless mass. Above this mass was a stratum of the largely immigrant urban proletariat, and above them the middle class, consisting of both immigrants and the descendants of Portuguese conquerors. The weaving of heimat was mainly the preoccupation of the middle class. The question that faced them was this: to whom should we address ourselves? To the workers in the cities, which would make them class conscious? Or to the passive masses, in order to include them in the fabric of society? Each precluded the other. To mobilize those living in the cities, they would have to be politicized; to approach the masses, one would have to deliver economic improvements and depoliticize them. The choice was whether to promote freedom or to fight hunger and disease. It is very difficult to see one's way clear when making such an impossible choice. I tried and failed.

Proponents of the "populist" tendency, who came to power with Vargas,[†] and whose last representative was the president who died be-

---

*Portuguese: "out-of-phase-ness, disconnection."

[†]Getulio Dornelles Vargas (1883–1954), Brazilian politician and president (1930–45 and 1951–54).

fore taking office, believed that they could evade this choice. First, the workers had to be politically mobilized in order to then be able to absorb the broad masses. This led to fascistic demagoguery and the vulgarization of all cultural life. The second, or "technocratic," tendency took the bull by the horns. According to proponents of this position, the first thing to be done was to alleviate poverty, and this required central planning. Such planning presupposes dictatorship and a "temporary" ban on all social, political, and cultural movement that might run counter to plan. This "technocratic" tendency was embodied in the army, an organization consisting of citizens. After 1964 it became clear to me that a technocratic victory over *populismo* was the only path that would finally allow Brazil to become a heimat. And it also became clear to me how this heimat would look: a gigantic advanced bureaucratic apparatus that would be second to none in its narrow-mindedness, fanaticism, and patriotic prejudice. Nevertheless, it took me until 1972 to make the painful decision to end my engagement with Brazil and to move to Provence, a sort of anti-Brazil.

⚜ ⚜ ⚜   My great disillusionment with Brazil was the discovery that each heimat, whether one has entered it through birth or is involved in its creation, is nothing but the enshrinement of banality, that heimat, however formed, is nothing but a home encased in mystification. And if one wishes to retain the freedom from heimat that one has gained in suffering, one must reject this mystification of customs and habits. My experience with Brazil has taught me that I must maintain the relationships that I entered into there, because I bear responsibility for my Brazilian compatriots, as they bear responsibility for me. I must now enter into new relationships outside Brazil and incorporate my Brazilian experience into these. Brazil is not my heimat; for me, heimat consists of the people for whom I choose to be responsible.

This is why the freedom won at the expense of heimat is not to be confused with philanthropy, cosmopolitanism, or humanism. I am not responsible for all humanity—or for, say, a billion Chinese. Rather, it is the freedom of responsibility for one's neighbor. It is the freedom that the Judeo-Christian tradition means when it calls on us to love our neighbor and says of the expellee who has been driven into the world that he must seek his heimat elsewhere.

⚘ ⚘ ⚘   People think of heimat as being a relatively permanent place; a home, as temporary and interchangeable. Actually, the opposite is true: one can exchange heimats—or have none at all—but one must always live somewhere, regardless of where. Parisian *clochards* live under bridges, Gypsies live in caravans, Brazilian agricultural workers live in huts, and as horrible as it may sound, people lived at Auschwitz. Because a person will simply perish without a home, a place to live. This death may be formulated in any number of ways, but the one that is least emotionally loaded is that without a place to live, without the protection of the usual and habitual, everything that encroaches on one is noise—without information—and without information, in a chaotic world, one can neither feel nor think nor act.

I built a house for myself in Robion. My desk is in the center of the house, surrounded by the customary disorder of my books and papers. The village to which I have become accustomed is outside my door, as is the post office and the weather, which I have also come to take for granted. Beyond them stretches increasingly unfamiliar territory: Provence, France, Europe, the earth, the expanding universe. But there is also the past year, lost heimats, the abysses of history and prehistory, the future that beckons adventurously, and the vast future that is unknown. I am embedded in the familiar so that I can reach out toward the unfamiliar and create things yet unknown. I am embedded in redundancy so that I can receive noise as information and so that I can produce information. My home, this network of the customary and familiar, serves to capture adventure and provides a springboard into adventure.

This dialectic between one's home and the unfamiliar [*Wohnung und Ungewöhnlichem*], between redundancy and noise is, according to a Hegelian analysis, the dynamic of the unhappy state of consciousness, which to all intents and purposes is consciousness itself. Consciousness is this oscillation between the familiar and the unfamiliar, between private and public. Hegel says that I lose myself when I discover the world, and I lose the world when I find myself. Without a place to dwell I would be unconscious, which means that without a place to dwell I would not be. Dwelling is the foundation of my existence in the world; it is fundamental.

But there is more than just the dialectic between the home and the world, between the familiar and the unfamiliar. There is also a dialectic inherent in the home, in the familiar itself. By the act of remaining open to the unfamiliar, by allowing the unfamiliar to be perceived as information, habit and custom themselves become closed to perception. When I sit at my desk, I don't see the papers and books that are lying all about because I'm used to them. But I do take note of the new books and correspondence that arrive. Habituation covers all phenomena like a blanket of cotton wool. It smoothes the sharp edges of all phenomena that it covers so that I no longer bump against them, but I am able to make use of them blindly. It is a little like the well-known Heidegger experiment of the slippers under the bed.* I don't perceive my home, but I do sense it dimly, and this dim sensation is called pretty, pleasant, or nice in aesthetics. All people have that sense of their own homes because they are used to them. This may be expressed in the aesthetic cycle: ugly-beautiful-pretty-ugly. Sounds that encroach on a home are ugly because they disturb the usual course of things. Once they have been processed and turned into information, they become beautiful because they are incorporated into the home. Through habituation this beauty is transformed into prettiness, because it is perceived only dimly. And finally, the home expels all that is superfluous, and those things become ugly again.

This digression into aesthetics was necessary in order to reach an understanding of love of heimat (or *Vaterland/patria*). Those who are settled in a place confuse heimat with home. Because of this they sense their heimat as nice and pleasant, in the same way as we do our homes. And then they confuse prettiness with beauty. The reason for this confusion is that they are enmeshed in their heimat, and so they are unable to transform the ugliness that approaches or touches them into

---

*Here Flusser is most likely referring to Heidegger's famous treatment of Van Gogh's painting *A Pair of Shoes* (1886 or 1887) in his essay "The Origin of the Work of Art" ("Vom Ursprung des Kunstwerkes" [1935–36]), published in Martin Heidegger, *Poetry, Language, Thought* (New York: Perennial Library, 1975).

something that is perhaps beautiful. Patriotism is symptomatic of a diseased aesthetic.

In some heimats, however, this prettiness that is mistaken for beauty, this confusion between the unfamiliar and the familiar, between the extraordinary and the ordinary, is not merely an aesthetic catastrophe but an ethical one as well. If I say that Provence or the Allgäu is beautiful, and I say this not because I have discovered these regions but because I have become used to them, then I am the victim of an aesthetic but not necessarily ethical error. But if I say that São Paulo is beautiful, then I am committing a sin, because my habits of thought, which obscure all phenomena, keep me from perceiving clearly the misery and injustice that exists there. I recognize them only dimly, and they become a part of the prettiness and niceness of that heimat, which I now see as beautiful. That is what is so catastrophic about habit.

A home is the foundation of all consciousness because it permits us to perceive the world. But dwelling is also anesthetizing because it itself is not perceived but only dimly sensed. This internal contradiction becomes even clearer when one confuses dwelling with heimat and the primary with the secondary. Because the settled person is so enmeshed in his heimat, it requires a conscious effort to perceive the world out there.

❦ ❦ ❦   Although the migrant, this human representative of a beckoning future without heimat, carries in his unconscious bits and pieces of the mysteries of all the heimats through which he has wandered, he is not anchored in any of them. In this sense he is a being lacking in mysteries. He becomes transparent to others. He lives in the clarity of the fact of being, not in mysteries. He is both a window through which those who have been left behind may see the world and the mirror in which they may see themselves, even if in distortion. But it is precisely this lack of mysteries that makes the migrant disturbing. The migrant's undeniable clarity and the foreigner's undeniable ugliness, which intrude on all heimats from all directions, place that heimat's prettiness and beauty in question. And because the resident confuses heimat with home, they also place in question his consciousness and even his existence in the world. What is disturbing about those who lack heimat is that they provide clear evidence, not that there are innumerable other heimats and mysteries, but that in the near future there may possibly be no mysteries of this sort at all.

The fact of being in which one without heimat lives presents him with a challenge, but not with something that is necessarily disturbing. The loss of the original, dimly sensed mystery of heimat has opened him up to a different sort of mystery: the mystery of living together with others. His challenge may be expressed as follows: how can I overcome the prejudices of the bits and pieces of mysteries that reside within me, and how can I break through the prejudices that are anchored in the mysteries of others, so that together with them we may create something beautiful out of something that is ugly? In this sense each person who is without heimat has at least the potential of representing the awakened consciousness of all those who are settled in a heimat. He can be a vanguard of the future. And it seems to me that we migrants must take this function on ourselves as our profession and calling.

❦ ❦ ❦ On the Alien

Whenever we pose existential questions, we confront the Alien. Who am I? Where am I? Where do I come from? Where am I going? These are all questions with which the "Alien" confronts me. Questions of identity and difference cannot be posed separately. There is an enormous literature on this subject, but the subject is inexhaustible. It is inexhaustible because the crisis of identity is permanent. The act of self-identification constantly throws one into crisis, because self-identification requires one to differentiate oneself from others, to discriminate against others. The words *crisis, criticism, criterion,* and *crimen* are all derived from a single root meaning "to differentiate." Identity is thus the consequence of a crisis, a criticism—a "crime" in the precise meaning of the word. "Who am I?" is a criminal question.

The criminal aspect of self-determination is not emphasized in the literature. That assertions such as "I am a father, a German, a Christian" are criminal is generally not brought up. It appears that there is a silent conspiracy to suppress this crime. René Girard recently published a book, *Le Bouc émissaire,** which treats the criminal side of self-determination. It examines how societies and individuals form identities. It examines discrimination against the Alien. The book makes for disturbing reading.

Its thesis is as follows. Every society (and each individual) is subject to crises. These crises—such as plagues, droughts, earthquakes—dissolve the order that regulates relationships among people. Society is thus transformed into an amorphous mass. All distinctions disappear: parents devour their children; sons rape their mothers; humans couple with animals. Wherever distinctions disappear, so do identities.

*René Girard, *The Scapegoat* (Baltimore, Md.: Johns Hopkins University Press, 1989).

Nobody knows who he is or what his place is. In such a critical situation it is pointless to look for the cause of the crisis. There would be no advantage to discovering what or who brought on a plague; the dissolution of the social order would in any case make it impossible to fight the cause. What is needed is to find some*one* to blame for the crisis. Having done so, the masses can then attack the guilty. The crisis is surmounted by means of mass murder, because the guilty are the ones who are differentiated from the mass. And as soon as difference is reestablished, identity once again becomes possible. Mass murder forms the basis of a new order.

This is what gives the guilty, the Alien, the "scapegoat" that ambiguity that is peculiar to all saints. Because in his guilt he is to blame for the crisis and the chaos, the scapegoat is devilish; because he is the founder of the new order, of the cosmos, he is divine. The Alien is holy because he negates me while at the same time allowing me to affirm myself. According to Girard this ambiguity in the saint, the Alien, forms the basis of all religious experience. All myths, from the most primitive to those that express themselves in present-day ideologies, conceal the scapegoat at their core. They are all myths of the scapegoat. Myths of self-determination.

If one wishes to pry the scapegoat from this core, however, one must first expose the myths and ideologies. None of them speaks of the scapegoat, the innocent victim, as such. To the contrary, they all speak of the guilty Alien, of an Alien whose guilt no one, not even he himself, doubts. In myth Oedipus is presented not as a scapegoat but rather as the one who brought down the plague on Thebes by sleeping with his mother and killing his father. And he did this because he was different from other Thebans; he was an Alien: he limped. It is not the myth itself but the analysis thereof that identifies the scapegoat in the myth. This is true of all myths, of African, Indian, Germanic, and Mexican ones, as well as of those that currently motivate our own deeds and experiences.

☙ ☙ ☙   As an example of the way mythical thinking operates, the author offers the "explanation" given for the plague by the fourteenth-century composer, canon, and royal adviser Guillaume de Machaut.

The Jews were to blame for the plague; it was they who poisoned the streams. However, there was no stockpile of toxins in the fourteenth century to poison all the streams. Nor did the plague abate after the Jews were exterminated; rather, it grew in virulence. And the Jews had suffered from the plague to the same extent as others. Machaut knew all this, but it did not hinder him in the least from pronouncing his explanation for the plague. Fundamentally, his explanation was not about the cause but rather about blame for the plague. He wasn't "lying"; he was thinking mythically and ideologically. It is only the critical historian who recognizes the scapegoat in Machaut's Jew, because he thinks causally, not mythically. Girard then asks: What enables the critic to think unmythically?

Before attempting to answer this question, he gives us something else to consider. It might appear that Machaut was not in any way responsible for the deaths of the Jews, precisely because he was thinking mythically, not causally. This would be an error. Machaut, the Thebans, and the Mexicans are all criminals who suppressed consciousness of their crimes in themselves and in others. Mythical consciousness is a criminal consciousness. The proof of this is the history of myth, since myths are not rigid constructions but rather change and have a history. And they all develop in the same direction. They all suppress the mass murder of the scapegoat that they originally extolled. In the foundation myth Romulus was murdered by the masses; in later versions he disappeared into the clouds. In the foundation myth Baldur was murdered by the masses; in later versions he died accidentally. Foundation myths (Kronos, etc.) are blood-thirsty, while later versions have passed through a poetic and aesthetic cleansing. The same applies to rites, which are the stagings of myths. The Mexican rites in which the hearts of living victims are torn out are more primal than the rites of the classical Greeks. Mythic consciousness has a bad conscience, and those ethnologists who defend the "noble savages" do so because they also suffer from a guilty conscience. We all do, because we all know that for us to affirm ourselves, we have to have murdered an innocent Alien.

And yet the responsibility of a Machaut (or of a Hitler) for the murder of the Alien is different from that of the Thebans or Mexicans, because neither Machaut nor Hitler could suppress consciousness of the murdered scapegoat in the same way as the Thebans and Mexicans could. This is because they possessed a model, Christianity, that did not permit them to do so. The Gospels are the exact opposite of myths: they are antimyths. They are a critique of myth. Whereas myths proclaim the guilt of the victim, the Gospels proclaim his innocence. Because myths do, in fact, understand the innocence of the victims (they suppress it, after all), the Gospels represent the revelation of that which the myths suppress. The thrust of Christianity is to destroy the myths by revealing what is covered up by them—to replace mythical consciousness with something else. Because of Christianity Machaut (and Hitler) were both capable of thinking unmythically, but they acted mythically nonetheless.

The Christian Gospel penetrates consciousness only weakly. We all still act mythically: we blame others so that we may affirm ourselves. At the same time we are capable of criticizing our mythical crimes from a Christian perspective. This is what gives the present age its characteristic tension: the more guilty our consciences, the more brutal our crimes become.

An example will illuminate this inner dialectic of ours: we attempt to remythify Christianity by claiming that the Jews crucified Christ. By doing so we hope to transform a murderous mass into a guilty victim. But at the same time we are aware of having turned Christianity on its head. The Gospels state that *all* crucified Christ, and continue to crucify him, and that *no one* recognizes his own guilt. The claim that the Jews crucified Christ is itself a crucifixion of Christ, and we are well-aware of this when we murder Jews.

To summarize the author's argument: There are "foundational," chaotic situations in which all differences vanish. In such situations we look for the Alien, the sinister, the uncanny, the scapegoat, in order to reestablish difference. We search out the monstrous. And in this search any anomaly will do: limping, hair color, foreign language. Once we have reestablished difference, we are again able to give ourselves identity. The scapegoat is the ab*norm*al, the *enorm*ous, while we ourselves are the norm. However, the tension between difference and identity leads to sanctification of the Alien. It represents both the destruction and the foundation of order. All religiosity before Christianity is sanctification of the Alien, of that which is totally "Other."

Christianity desanctifies the Alien in that it makes clear that he *is* a scapegoat: as the paschal lamb and as the bearer of sins. It does so by revealing the dialogic function of identification. We identify ourselves as the Other of the Other. The Alien is no longer an "it," an object that is different from us and therefore gives us identity. Rather, the Alien is a "you" who addresses us as "you" and thereby allows us to call ourselves "I." Christianity replaces persecution with dialogue, hatred with love. It is not the Alien that is sacred but the relationship of dialogue. This is how Christianity opens the way to unmythicized, causal, and scientific thinking and gives us the capacity to criticize myths and ideologies. We have barely begun to walk along this path.

❦ ❦ ❦   We Need a Philosophy
of Emigration

Humans are contingent [*bedingt*] beings, and the things that make
them contingent may be classified. For example, we may posit a class
of natural and a class of man-made things. One can then say that humans are contingent on the nature and culture in which they find
themselves. To be contingent means being surrounded by things that
steer the movement of the contingent being along certain pathways.
Humans are contingent beings because their movements are directed
along certain pathways by natural and cultural things in their surroundings. Contingence [*Bedingung*] is an explanation by that which
is contingent because it is only as a result of the contingence that the
pathways through which the contingence is directed are glimpsed, so
that this passage may be predicted. Human beings may be explained
in terms of their natural and cultural contingence.

But humans are not completely contingent. There is in their surroundings one place without things. From the vantage point of this
place a person may gain an overview of his surroundings. If this place
did not exist, the previous lines could not have been written. This place
that is free of things may be called the ironic. When we take an ironic
stance, we are afforded a clearer view of our contingence. A person's
movement into and out of irony cannot be foreseen from the vantage
point of his contingence. Human beings are not completely explicable
from their contingence.

The movement into irony is an act of outrage. And with this motion a person rises above contingence. Movement away from irony is
a form of engagement. With this motion the person returns to his state
of contingence to change it. These two movements taken together are
called freedom. Human beings are free because with this inexplicable

and unpredictable movement they are able to become outraged about their contingence and to change it. Because of this potential we are virtually free, and when we complete this action we are free in fact.

This potential for moving into and out of irony is what differentiates human beings from the things in their surroundings. It represents their dignity. Every attempt to explain human beings, whether from the vantage point of their natural or cultural contingence, degrades them. However, natural explanations of humans degrade them more than do cultural ones because they point out the absurdity of this outrage. It is far more absurd for me to become outraged at my contingence as a mammal than to do so at my contingence as a member of the middle class. True, I am both mammal and middle class, even though I was never asked whether I wanted to be either. So both degrade me. But it seems more promising to me to become outraged at my middle-classness than my mammalianism, because I have a better chance of changing the former. This is also why fascistoid explanations of human beings are a greater debasement than those that are socialistoid. Nevertheless, they are false explanations, because they suppress what is inexplicable about human beings, namely, their dignity.

I could also call this outrage in irony "emigration" and the reverse movement out of irony (engagement) "immigration." By coining this new terminology, I am shifting the problem a little. And I am doing so in two ways: in my outrage I emigrate out of one contingence to immigrate into another, but my emigration is not only a matter of outrage; it is also a form of flight. The shift of this problem should be viewed in this light.

It is possible for me to change my contingence by exchanging it. This exchange is itself a change, because the contingence I have left is different because of my having left, and the contingence that I have entered is different because of my having entered. However, this type of change has a different valence than does a return to the original contingence—the valence of flight. I give up my initial contingence in flight, and I seek refuge in another one. Is that still a form of outrage and engagement in the true sense of the word? Can one still talk of freedom in such a case? Is a person free simply because he is able to flee? I believe that this question may be answered structurally. When I leave the first contingence so that I may enter another one at the same level, I am a refugee. I have become neither outraged nor engaged but have allowed myself to drift. There is no dignity in such movement. However, if I leave the first contingence and enter into a state of irony, and then enter the second contingence out of this irony, then I am both outraged and engaged, and my decision has dignity.

The theoretical difference between flight and genuine emigration, and between refuge and genuine immigration, is relatively simple. The practical difference is more difficult to define. As a practical matter flight is an element of every emigration, and refuge, an element of every immigration. Conversely, there is an element of emigration in every flight, even though refuge usually lacks engagement. But in practice there are certain signs that may help us to mark the difference.

What differentiates the emigrant from the refugee? For better or worse the refugee is stuck in the contingence he has left behind. He carries it inside him on his travels with a mixture of resentfulness and love. The emigrant, on the other hand, has risen above that contingence. In his outrage he is able to hold onto things that he values and reject others. What differentiates the immigrant from the refugee? The refugee, who is cocooned in the old contingence, is closed to the new. He can neither contribute anything to it nor take anything from it. The immigrant, on the other hand, is partially opened to the new contingence, precisely at those points where the old contingence has been ironically rejected. At these points he is able to assimilate the new contingence and assimilate himself into it. And at those points where he chooses to retain pieces of his old contingence, he is able to act on the new one as well.

There is also such a thing as internal emigration; the author has not experienced this, however, and so cannot assess it. It is his hope that he is an emigrant from Europe and an immigrant to Brazil. It cannot be denied that the structure of what he left behind and the contingence that he entered into affect both his emigration and his immigration. Humans are still at least partially contingent beings. The structure of European contingence is such that it makes it easier for the determined emigrant to be outraged. The structure of Brazilian contingence is such that it makes it easier for the determined immigrant to become engaged. Nevertheless, the decision is always a difficult one because the ties of contingence always cleave to people. It is always easier to be a refugee and to veil flight with the concept of loyalty. True loyalty is engagement with that which is freely chosen. In other words, the concept of loyalty cannot be separated from that of freedom. The loyalty of the refugee is a false loyalty. The person who slavishly holds to a European contingence in Brazil is not truly loyal to that contingence. Rather, it is the one who tries to incorporate parts of this contingence into Brazilian life who is loyal, even though his engagement is with Brazil and not with Europe.

A philosophy of emigration is still to be written. Its categories are still nebulous and blurred. But it needs to be written because it would benefit not only actual emigrants but virtual ones as well. One of its principal tasks would have to be to differentiate as clearly as possible between emigration and flight in a world in which many are forced to flee.

❦ ❦ ❦ To Be Unsettled, One First Has to Be Settled

People are generally expelled from someplace to nowhere in particular. If they don't perish in the process, they become immigrants somewhere. Even though expulsions have occurred ever since human beings became settled, they remain horrific. All three phases of the process are unsettling: being expelled, wandering in the void, and finally, being beached somewhere. The first phase unsettles us out of the ground that supports our reality; the second exposes us to unreality; the third transports us into an unacceptable second-degree reality. This desettling and unsettling are usually viewed negatively. In this essay I will try to tease positive aspects from them.

To be unsettled, one first has to be settled somewhere. There is nothing self-evident about this. To the contrary, superficially the difference between plants and animals is that animals are not settled but rather laid down or dropped. From the point of view of plants, animals are unsettled beings and therefore unsettling. Just how this looks from the viewpoint of animals is hard to imagine because, unlike plants, animals don't really have a single viewpoint. What they do have are points where they lie down and paths along which they move; they are seldom stationary, standing on one point. And human beings are extraordinarily restless animals. Not only are they constantly on the move, but they gather and transmit experience. Human beings are even more rootless than other animals, and when they do search out their roots, one gets a vegetable impression of them. Truly rooted and settled people (to the extent they exist in reality and not just in ideology) are experientially impoverished shrubs. To be a human being in the true sense of the word, one has to be unsettled. According to Aristotle, the starting point of philosophy has always been unsettledness. And because people only seldom allow themselves to become unsettled, being expelled is a good way of becoming a human being in the full sense of the word.

It may be argued that this method seems a little too radical (i.e., at root). Wouldn't it be possible to travel about gathering experience and then return to the campfire [*Lagerfeuer*] (home) to work through what one has experienced? And then to store it [*lagern*]? Rather as Indians in children's stories do? Or as tourists do, according to travel agencies? Why 3 million expelled Afghans instead of 20 million vacation travelers? Do Afghans, in fact, philosophize better than do tourists? The answer is that it may well be that expulsion is too radical when compared to tourism and that neither of these alternatives necessarily yields human beings in the full sense of the word. But expulsion exists along with tourism, and we must try to make the best of it. This is not an argument in favor of either expulsion or tourism, but it is aimed at expellees, who have the potential of making something out of their unsettledness.

The fact that there are expellees presupposes that there are expellers, people who think of themselves as vegetables (as native) but behave like rats. They expel anyone who does not accord with their putative point of view, so that it will not become apparent that it is no point of view at all but rather an empty refuge in which the same pups are whelped over and over again. They expel the rejects [*Auswurf*] so that their spawn [*Wurf*] always remain the same. Those who are expelled are always the rejects of the identical spawn; they are an elite created by those who expel them. But they shouldn't have any illusions about the noblesse oblige of the latter: they have been ennobled not as a result of anything they *did* but only by those who drove them out. Nevertheless, their situation is one of "noblesse oblige": they have an obligation to the condition of their own expulsion. They may not permit themselves to be merely driven, for otherwise they become mere flotsam. They must attempt to experience, identify, and assess their expulsion as a sort of stimulus. If they succeed in this, their unsettledness will be transformed into resolve. They may then become human beings in the full sense of the word: animals that act with resolve, even though they are as yet unaware of the end toward which they strive.

If we consider what I have written—and suppress counterarguments—one must conclude that "human being in the fullest sense" and "expellee" are synonyms. We are all expellees to the extent that we unsettle ourselves, when our seatedness in habit is continually exorcised. This would seem to make harmless that which is unsettling in expulsion, because it would become banal and routine. And the claim that we are all expellees (e-stranged beings) is also so banal that one might well forget what sort of unsettledness it expresses. But I'm not talking about this banality here. What I mean is that we may easily recognize ourselves in the expellee and his unsettledness. They are just like us, except more so. We also experience three phases: the loss of ground under our feet, the unreality around us and within us, and the unacceptable second-degree reality. We merely experience these in less obvious ways. And so we may perhaps say the following: the expellees whom we occasionally see on television show us that to which we would do well to aspire.

❦ ❦ ❦   Planning the Unplannable*

Let me posit that "tourism" is travel for travel's sake and offer the thesis that at present tourism plays a role approximately analogous to that played by theory in antiquity. *Theory* is a little like *sight-seeing* (being a spectator of the sight-worthy), and classical theory differs from its modern counterpart in that it is pure—it was never its purpose to be applied. Modern tourism and classical theory have in common a gratuitous purposelessness as catharsis, and it is impossible to understand the present—or see into the future—without taking the phenomenon of tourism seriously. A phenomenology of tourism has yet to be written. The purpose of this essay is to suggest the possible contours of such a study.

Perspectives on tourism that come from outside tourism are to be rejected—for example, the point of view of the tourism industry (on which a number of European countries are dependent), national governments (according to the press, the army of tourists was the French government's biggest worry at the beginning of July), international politics (the porosity of national borders and their disintegration will increase traffic among them and lead to the downfall of nationalism and then of nationality itself), ethnology (the dislocation of folk customs, so that Americans wear lederhosen and Bavarians wear bermudas), linguistics (the osmosis of particles, reminiscent of Japan, from completely unrelated languages, so that Catalonians talk of snack bars and Bavarians, of *dachas*), and so on. All these perspectives are to be jettisoned in favor of that of tourism itself, and this perspective should be taken as if one were an astonished person from an underdeveloped

---

*German: "Planung des Planlosen." Strictly speaking, *planlos* means simply "without plan" and does not imply something that cannot be planned, that is, something that is "unplannable."

country. As Aristotle pointed out, surprise has always been a goad to philosophizing.

❦ ❦ ❦   Tourism has three phases: departure, the trip itself, and the return home. Once upon a time departure was attended by an almost mythical solemnity of annual cyclical return, as well as of adventure. Maps were studied, itineraries compared, hotel reservations arranged, and clothing bought. Plans were carefully made. Vacations punctuated the year, much as pilgrimages did the Middle Ages and mysteries and games did the ancient world. Those who stayed behind accompanied tourists to the train station, a solemn entourage complete with advice, tears, smiles, and waving hankies. Today things are thrown helter-skelter into the back of the car at the end of the workday or on the last day of school (it goes without saying that even schoolmates have cars these days), and if one forgets something, it can be bought at the same price and quality almost anywhere. The formalities of currency exchange, passports, and visas have shrunk to the point of triviality, and the main obstacle is the decision to go or not to go. Because of this departures are quick. And still there is something solemn about them: everyday experience is left behind in the gray fog of a past transcended. One's own town is transformed into circumstances suffered through; responsibilities dissolve; even one's place of dwelling becomes strange. Departure is a liberation from habit, and in the decision to depart one seizes at a fundamental freedom—the freedom of movement. Without that freedom life would no longer be worth living. Recently a young West Berliner told me that what he felt even more than the strictures created by the Wall was the circumstance of having to travel many hours before being able to travel without itinerary or plan. Lack of planning, the *acte gratuite,* is the essence of the freedom of movement. It is the essence of tourism. But of course, we must also take into account that, dialectically, this planless freedom is now preplanned by the liberal capitalism that has triumphed throughout Europe. This is an unsettling fact.

There is, however, no such thing as a decision made in the absence of planning. Often all one has to do is glance at the roofs of cars to draw certain conclusions about the intentions of its occupants: baby carriages, tents, skis, sailboats (car roofs as a contribution to the Hegelian dialectic of freedom). And even though the European highway system is extremely dense, it nevertheless regulates movement. (If "freedom" is defined as the number of available alternatives, the density of the highway system is an indicator of freedom.) Everywhere one looks, the unintentional is being planned for. For a South American the density of the highway system has an even greater effect, given the diversity of landscapes encompassed by it. Drive just a few kilometers, and the scenery is completely changed. The cultural and natural surroundings of Asturia are completely different from Galicia and the Basque country, Languedoc differs from Rousillon and Provence, Oberammergau from Pinzgau, and yet for South America these are ridiculously small distances. Existentially a 50-kilometer drive in Europe corresponds to 500 kilometers in Brazil, given the scale of the country. True, the waves of tourists that have flooded Europe have blurred all regionalism, yet tourism has served as a catalyst, encouraging the emergence of an artificial regionalism. (Again, a dialectic.) A man from Provence may tour Norway or Turkey—which undoubtedly does nothing to further his provincialism—and he may eat cod and shishkebob at home, but he will serve a Scottish visitor to Provence trout with almonds and white wine, even as he swaps impressions of Cadiz with him over the meal.

To a visitor from the New World the roads are surprisingly free of billboards, leaving wide vistas open to the eye. But the roads do pass by an abundance of signs announcing "Chambres, Rooms, Zimmer, Stanze" and the like. The prices quoted may vary considerably, but the quality is almost uniformly good, and price criteria do not determine tourists' choices of where to stay. Proletarians who have recently entered the middle class and upper-class arrivistes choose on the basis of criteria that seem opaque to the outsider, mirroring in their choice of accommodations gradations in social class that are in the process of being overhauled. It is, on the whole, hard to discern social differences among tourists. They wear the same clothes and drive the same cars; only facial expressions and a few mannerisms give anything away. Europeans themselves are perhaps better able to differentiate, apparently noting that ex-proletarians are even more wasteful than ex-members of the middle class. For example, the latter seem to favor the back rows of theaters. We have to recognize that economic criteria no longer serve to separate the classes and that in the future it may no longer be necessary or interesting to attempt such a division. What motivates tourists to choose this or that place is indeterminate; the decisive factor in the decision is chance. This element of chance gives tourism a gamelike quality so that the tourist may represent a recent hominid ancestor of an emerging *Homo ludens.** (The aleatory negentropy within the entropically planned world of neocapitalism as habitat of the absurd, or of man the game player.) Even though chance governs the Brownian motion of tourism,[†] there is nonetheless a discernible goal: aloneness and community. No one from the Americas needs to be told that community can flourish only against a backdrop of aloneness and that amorphous masses thwart human relationship. Although massification in Europe has not yet reached American proportions, tourism is a phenomenon rooted in massification and attempts to overcome it. And so small, temporary communities emerge at inns and campgrounds in secluded places on mountaintops, beaches, lakes, and ponds. These communities, made up of multinational and heterogeneous elements, are thrown together by chance, and this is where a new hierarchy of choice involving noneconomic criteria is being elaborated. This is the new *polis,* and it awaits a Plato to make it a utopia. The characteristic "open structure" of these play communes is underscored by the nomadic procession of tourists that makes communities as changeable as oases, so that while their form (parking lot) remains constant, the camels (motor homes, campers) change. Communications theory has a good deal of catching up to do in the area of tourism.

Augmenting the open communities are a variety of archaic holdovers, such as spas and vacation hotels, that maintain a Victorian char-

---

*Latin: "playful human." Flusser is most likely referring to *Homo ludens: Proeve eener bepaling van het spelelement der cultuur* (*Homo Ludens: A Study of the Play-Element in Culture* [New York: Roy, 1950]) by the Dutch historian Johan Huizinga, published in 1930.

[†]Robert Brown (1773–1858), a Scottish botanist, discovered what later came to be called Brownian motion in 1827 by observing that microscopic pollen grains move about randomly in water.

acter—a sort of art museum of the good old days. The vast majority of older European men and women who not only refuse to die but insist on enjoying their old age swear by the atmosphere of nature preserves (culture as nature). The large number of war injured among them attests to the character of those good old days. It is well to preserve this cultural panopticon lest the young forget.

And then the electronic horns signal the return home. This taps, which the planned world blows for the future *Homo ludens,* effects a sort of transformation. The tourist's car is changed from a freedom machine back into mere transportation; his wife is transformed again from a companion into a cook and nursemaid; his children change from playmates into invisible "expenses" in the appropriate budget column; and he himself is turned from a near-human back into a consumer, taxpayer, and productive element of society. This occurs with the following burdensome circumstance: the ex-tourist returns to the encapsulation of home from a state of temporary transcendence, and so he sees his abasement from outside and therefore better. It doesn't help to know that a period of functioning will again be followed by a period of tourism and that there is a tendency to disparage the period of functioning. It needs to be recognized that tourism is founded on functioning and that the functionary lies at the heart of the tourist. The young people who are now protesting may perhaps be characterized as follows: they are tourists who wish to deny the functionary within themselves and without and refuse to go home. Tourism is thus an achievement of planned liberalism in which the dangerous dialectic of freedom becomes especially evident.

At the beginning of this essay, I stated that today tourism plays approximately the same role as theory did in antiquity. Both—modern tourism and Greek philosophy—turn their backs on economics and politics and seek purity of vision and the playful act. After the catharsis, both are plunged back into the Platonic cave. But there are important differences. For example, the Greek philosopher was an aristocrat in that slaves and artisans were *beneath* him; the modern tourist carries the functionary and voter *within* himself, which makes him a democrat. Another difference is that the philosopher takes a journey into the sublime; the tourist, into the absurd. Many other differences could be listed. Tourism may possibly be envisioned in the light of its parallels to philosophy, but these cannot help us understand or explain it. It is sufficiently mysterious that, even if one were to take it as a harbinger of the future, that future should be ceded to the opacity of mystery.

⚘ ⚘ ⚘ From Guest to Guest Worker

"Guests" who visit Europe infrequently or come from great distances may take note not only of the institution of the guest worker but also of this strange word, which was coined in German-speaking countries.* True, linguistic mystification and euphemism are practiced everywhere. Nevertheless, this one is characteristic of our general condition. It evokes the concept of the "guest," which is sanctified in all primitive cultures, and the concept of the "worker," a term that has been celebrated since about the nineteenth century, to quiet possibly troubled consciences. It may be that this term points to a fundamental development in our culture from guest to guest worker.

The guest is a constant figure in all myths, and hospitality is an integral part of all rites. The explanation may be as follows. Primitive man lives in underpopulated and relatively isolated societies (in tribes or villages). The members of his social group assume an importance for him that is much diluted in modern society. (This is one reason for our difficulty in understanding the concept of "neighbor" in the biblical sense.) Whenever a foreigner comes into this social group (and this happens only seldom), he appears alien, unusual, astonishing, suspicious—in short, "Other." However, all the previously mentioned characteristics are also typical of the divine. Hospitality is a part of the

*In the late fifties the German government issued an invitation to European countries such as Italy, Spain, Greece and Turkey to send so-called *Gastarbeiter*, or guest workers, to propel the booming German economy and alleviate the shortage of labor. In 1961 Turkey signed its first agreement with Germany to export labor. Alarmed by a recession, however, by 1973 Germany ended the call for immigrant workers, officially referred to as *"Anwerbestop"* (recruiting stoppage). The government mistakenly presumed that the *"Gastarbeiter"* would return home. Turkish immigrants today are by far the largest minority group in Germany, having settled with their families primarily in large cities such as Berlin and Frankfurt and in areas of heavy industrialization.

rite by which we attempt to assuage the "Other." That is why the biblical commandment that relates to the Sabbath explicitly mentions the guest and why the saying "a guest at home, God at home" is common to many peoples. It is also why the host in some cultures offers a guest not merely salt and bread but even his own wife for a night. So the dissolution of hospitality may serve as a measure of demythification in a society. For example, as one travels from the north of Brazil to the south (that is, in the direction of "development"), one observes that hospitality declines progressively. The formlessness with which we receive guests demonstrates our distance from the original mythical source of these rites, and the forms that we nonetheless retain demonstrate their staying power.

❦ ❦ ❦   The guest worker is the consequence of a peculiar circumstance: although the Industrial Revolution succeeded in replacing human beings with machines for highly complex industrial and agricultural manipulations, it did not succeed in replacing them economically in simple (and therefore degrading) ones. One aspect of freedom (a classical Marxist one) involves the liberation of human beings by means of machines. An associated apprehension (Nietzsche's, for example) is that extensive mechanization could lead to general unfreedom. (It should not come as a surprise that the New Left draws on Nietzsche. He is as little responsible for the abuse of his ideas by the prewar right wing as is Marx for the abuse of his ideas by Stalinism.) However, the guest worker hints at a problem that neither Nietzsche nor Marx recognized: a society freed by mechanization in which manual labor is imported to carry out primitive manipulations.

Technically the guest worker cannot be equated with the slave in the sense in which the word was used in Brazil in the nineteenth century. He freely enters into contractual agreement, the agreement is honored by the host, and after the term of the agreement has run out, he is free to go back home and take his earnings with him. However, several other points need to be made. In the first place, the agreement hardly gives the guest worker an adequate picture of the hospitality that awaits him. True, it guarantees him a particular wage, which may be many times what he could earn at home. But it withholds the information that living quarters are limited by prejudice and that rent will eat up a large part of his earnings because it has been inflated by speculation. It conceals that the cost of living will be many times what the guest worker expects. And that in spite of its hospitality, the host country will, in its blind impartiality, skim off a further portion of his earnings in the form of taxes, and that he will not be able to evade the tax man, as he could in his home country. And that even if he manages to save some money as a result of several years of self-abnegation, this money will have been saved at the cost of alienation once he returns home. In other contexts (such as the procurement of European prostitutes for Brazilian brothels at the beginning of the twentieth century) defective contracts like these are called "white slavery," and so perhaps the word *slavery* is not out of place after all.

Second, it should be noted that the guest worker is an odd sort of guest, an Other in the uncanny sense of the word. His mere existence in the host country; his appearance; his impoverishment, which sets him off from his surroundings; his gestures and doings, which proclaim his cultural foreignness—all these threaten to tear the well-woven but always defensive fabric of the surrounding society. It is therefore understandable that he should become the lightning rod for suppressed aggression (which can often be supported by objective facts), and this tendency is only intensified by the numerous efforts by well-intentioned persons to foster relations based on "human dignity."

Seen in this light, the development from guest to guest worker is an aspect of the development of interpersonal relationships in that culture we call "Western." The guest is a hierophant, a manifestation of the divine, the Other of human beings. The slave that develops from among a variety of possible outcomes represents the transformation of the guest into a thing of which I am the owner and of which I may dispose as I wish. But like all other possessions, it also has a value that must be maintained. Furthermore, the guest worker represents the transformation of the guest into a tool, which I may make use of as needed, whose work is so fleeting, so inconsequential, that there is no need for great distress.

Seen in this light, a solution to the problem of the guest worker can be approached not by ad hoc measures but only by a radical restructuring of interpersonal relationships. One thing seems clear: the wealth of Western Europe (this unique phenomenon in our history) is somehow put in question by the problem outlined here, and not just economically (that could certainly be solved) but morally. And the way in which the moral aspect of this problem is resolved will have momentous consequences for the future.

❦ ❦ ❦   Thinking about Nomadism

People throughout the world are beginning to give serious thought to nomads. Viewed externally, the explanation might be that people are scurrying about like ants on an ant hill, frightened into a frenzy of action by a transcendent foot. Such an unthinking rushing back and forth is not exactly what is meant by nomadism. True, people swarm to a variety of rhythms layered one atop the next (such as occurs daily in large cities, annually at beaches and ski slopes, or over a lifetime in the form of refugees and guest workers), and this grand rhythm is reminiscent of nomadic migrations across Asian steppes and African deserts. But even this lifelong migratory rhythm—let's say from the underdeveloped south toward the land of milk and honey—is not the same as the nomadic existence of Mongols, Bedouins, or Gypsies as we have come to perceive them. Because of this, the external explanation for the emergent interest in the nomadic is probably not appropriate. This interest is surfacing not because there are so many automobiles, refugees, and guest workers in the world, or because we ourselves are hopping about the world like fleas, but because something deeper is being stirred up.

From years of schooling we are used to dividing the span of human existence into epochs. We speak of the Stone Age, Copper Age, Bronze Age, and Iron Age—and perhaps even of a Modern Age. This classification is fascinating for at least two reasons. The first is that the material used to make tools (that is, culture) is the criterion for the classification. It is a tangible and concrete criterion—nothing soft and spongy like the division of modern times into the Renaissance, Baroque, and so on. Another reason for the fascination is the more than logarithmic scale at which the classification is calibrated. The Stone Age takes up approximately 2 million years; the Iron Age, at most 5,000 years. This scale was developed looking back from our position in the here and now, and seen from here, last year is just as long as the billions of years that transpired between the Big Bang and the origins of life on earth. What is fascinating about the span of human existence according to the classifications taught in middle school is their naive existential concreteness—refreshing in comparison to academic classifications. Unfortunately, it is impossible to maintain the naïveté of middle-school students. As a result, the classification of the span of human existence must be examined critically. The first thing one notices is that the word *stone* is not well defined. Aren't copper, bronze, and iron rocks? In that case, one would have to call virtually the entire time span the "Stone Age," with the exception of the last twenty to thirty years. But is that a sensible division: 2 million years of Stone Age and twenty years of a Nonmaterial Age? Some other way must be found. The Stone Age has to be divided. And in fact this is what is done in our middle schools: a division into the Paleolithic, Mesolithic, and Neolithic Ages. Except that now, after critical reflection, the classification looks something like this: the Paleolithic Age up to the invention of agriculture, and the Neolithic Age up to 1990. And this is precisely why interest in nomadism is surfacing right now.

⚲ ⚲ ⚲   What I just said is infuriating (if only because it attacks prejudices), and so it requires justification. Here is my attempt at doing so: the proposed three-part division of the span of human existence into Paleolithic Age, Neolithic Age, and the Immediate Future is based on the three catastrophes that we have experienced over the course of our existence. The first may be called "humanization," and it was characterized primarily by the use of stone tools. The second catastrophe may be called the "creation of civilization," and it has been characterized above all by life lived in settlements. The third one has as yet no fitting name; it is characterized primarily by the fact that our world of habit is becoming uninhabitable. If we accept the premise of these three catastrophes (even if only for as long as it takes to read this essay), then the following telling of human history becomes possible. Humankind in all its forms (including *Homo sapiens sapiens*) is a species of nomadic hunter-gatherers that differs from other species by its use of tools. Approximately 10,000 years ago there was an ecological disaster. The climate became warmer, and the steppes were transformed into forests. Instead of simply dying out in its hunter-gatherer ways, as it was supposed to, *Homo sapiens sapiens* transformed the forests back into steppes, and instead of continuing to hunt and gather, the species began to eat grasses and to keep grass-eating animals on this artificially created grassland. They turned from hunting and gathering to agriculture and animal breeding, becoming settled for this purpose. Today the surface of the planet (both forest and steppe) is only a sort of substrate for three- and multidimensional "nonmaterial" fields (such as electromagnetism), and we are now in the process of transforming our agricultural and breeding status into a new, but again nomadicizing, form of existence. What this means for our three-part division of human existence is that the Neolithic Age was a 10,000-year interruption in nomadic life.

But this still doesn't justify my premise, because the three catastrophes, whose existence I have asked you to accept (especially the third one), are all ad hoc hypotheses. And even granted that what we are calling the Neolithic Age (from about 8000 B.C. to 1990) is the period of settled civilization, what gives us the right to end that epoch in the year 1990? Where do we get our conviction that the period of civilization has come to an end (which is even more radical than the assumption of an impending posthistory)? After all, our currently developing *interest* in nomadism cannot sufficiently entitle us to such catastrophic diagnoses. What is clear is that we are caught in a vicious circle. To justify our interest in nomadism, we divide the span of human existence anew, and to justify this new classification, we call on our interest as evidence. We must break out of this circle. This can be done if the two forms of existence proposed here—nomadism and settledness—are first compared to each other phenomenologically and then integrated into the new classification. If this integration succeeds, we will see whether we are justified in our claim that the next catastrophe will be one of global uninhabitability.

❦ ❦ ❦   The settled are localized, and nomads wander. To begin with, this means that settled people may be located in space (that is, they have addresses), whereas nomads may be defined only along a space-time continuum. All that is needed to locate a settled person is to say that he lives at the corner of Fourth Avenue and Fifty-second Street in New York City. For a nomad you would also have to specify April 10, 1990, 4 P.M. From the spatial point of view of the settled, nomads are transitory phenomena; from the spatial-temporal perspective of the wanderer, settled people are amputees lacking in an important dimension of being. But this contradiction should not be carried to the extreme. The settled also have a temporal dimension because they live and must therefore also die. They are also transient phenomena or, to give it a medieval cast, *homines viatores** in the vale of tears that is this life. Because of this, the addresses of the settled must also be dated (for example, for the Romans, by saying who was consul at a particular time, or for Jesus, that he was killed under Pontius Pilate). On the other hand, nomads must encamp occasionally as well, because their bodies have weight. They, too, are cripples who are not simply free as the wind. Because of this, Ghengis Khan's grave and his yurt may be located geographically. In short, although the settled are localized and nomads wander, both conditions are contingent, because both are human beings.

And yet, those who are settled conduct their lives in a manner that is completely foreign to the wanderer. One simple but perhaps facile way of grasping this is to avail oneself of etymology. It is true that the settled possesses [*be-sitzt*] and the wanderer experiences [*er-fährt*], or that the settled inhabits the habitual and the wanderer lives dangerously [daß der Fahrende Gefahr läuft].† But no matter how correct the insight contained within the roots of these words, the phenomenon itself requires examination, not just wordplay. Looking at the phenomenon of settledness, one sees houses with stables and fields. One may see a village; in other words, one sees politically. The phenomenon of wandering is not as easily observed, however, because hunters wander differently than do herders or tourists. So, even though property developed hundreds of thousands of years later than experience, our con-

---

*Latin: "traveling humans."

†Literally: "runs dangers."

siderations must begin with settledness, because property is easier to observe than experience.

❧ ❧ ❧   A village may be thought of as a grouping of houses around a village square, with a hill rising above it and a stream flowing by it. (Of course, this vision represents the idealized village in a perfect republic.) But it immediately becomes apparent that the settled aren't simply sitting on their rear ends. They move about and have dealings with others. They go back and forth between their homes and the village square, walk up and down the hill, and go down to the stream to refill their buckets with water. The traffic that I have just described, and the police who regulate it, constitute what we call "civilized life," the word *civilized* meaning "village-dwelling."

This settled form of existence has been commented on endlessly, and what remains to be said might be virtually endless as well were it not spinning idly and in the process of dissolution. Because the fundamental question, "Why are these people rushing back and forth instead of sitting?" or to put it perhaps a little more nicely, "Why are they engaged politically instead of tending their gardens?" now has a definitive, if disappointing, answer: until now people could not gather information if they stayed at home. Until now those who never left their homes were seen as "idiots" in the original Greek sense of the word, that is, private people who knew nothing of the world. That has changed as a result of the Information Revolution. Information is now distributed to private homes, and presently it is the person who leaves his home and goes out in public who is seen as the idiot. It looks as if this rushing about is now purposeless and that it is now finally possible to remain seated.

But this would be an error, because the information that is delivered into the home must be carried by material or nonmaterial channels, which puncture roofs and walls. The home has become drafty, as gales of media sweep through from all directions: it has become uninhabitable. The most unusual thing about a house that has become unlivable is that nothing in it can actually be possessed [*be-sitzen*] because everything that is movable (furniture, chairs, etc.) and everything that is immovable (ground and floor) has been stirred up to the point where a division between private and public no longer makes sense. This unusual impossibility, staying seated (possessing) amid the media storm, may be formulated more clearly.

(1) It is information and not possessions (software not hardware) that empowers, and (2) communication, not economics, now forms the substructure of the village (society). What this two-part formulation makes clear is that the settled form of existence—the home—and a fortiori the stable, field, hill, and stream are no longer functional. In effect, we have begun to be nomadic. So, let us envisage nomads. Nomads are people who pursue some goal, whether gathering mushrooms, killing animals, or milking sheep, and so on. Whatever their goal, their wanderings do not come to an end when the goal has been achieved. All goals are way stations; they are situated next to the pathway (Greek *metodos*), and the wandering, taken as a whole, may be seen as an aimless method. In contrast to the back-and-forth rushing of settled people between the private and the political, the wandering of nomads is open-ended. This seemingly aimless wandering may, however, be an error of perspective on the part of the settled. We settled people have worked out the laws regulating our movements but not those relating to the sweep of wandering—just as we have worked out the laws regulating a falling stone but not the vagaries of the wind. It may be that the nomadic existence through steppe and across desert may have the same structure as cloud and wind, while the settled life of back and forth corresponds structurally to summer and winter. Perhaps nomads live meteorologically, and we, astronomically. Or maybe it would be more apt to say that the rhythms of settled life must be expressed by traditional algorithms; that of nomads, by fractal ones.

In any case, the wind is for the nomad what the ground is for the settled. What we settled people find uncomfortable about the wind is that although it may be felt, heard, and experienced, it is intangible—and incomprehensible. This physically experiential and yet intangible quality of the wind lends it an aura that we call "sacredness." There is something ghostly and spiritual about it, and it is closely related to breathing and speaking, these winds of the human spirit. In earlier times this groundless intangible experience was given names such as *ruach, pneuma,* or *spiritus;* today we speak of nonmaterial culture and software. In earlier times the wind was held to have a voice that called—a calling that beckoned. Today we deem as characteristic that the wind grinds the tangible, possessable ground into grains of sand (calculates), scatters them to the wind (disperses), and then piles them up in dunes (computes). The wind, this phantasmical intangibility that drives the nomad and whose call he obeys, is an experience that we describe in terms of calculus and computation. We are beginning to live the nomadic life not only because the wind blows through our punctured houses but in particular because it has entered into us.

The meteorological, "self-similar," fractal fact that the wind pulverizes, scatters, and then piles is not only a posthistorical discovery. For example, early Christianity spoke of a *logos spermatikos,* a "seed-scattering word," and the Jewish mystic, of a *galut leshechinah,* a "scattering of the spirit." Only now has the scattering of the spirit (diaspora) become central to ontological and anthropological thought. The world appears to us as a scattering of sand that is dispersed ever more evenly by the wind of entropy, through which dunes may form haphazardly. And human beings appear to us as the wind that intentionally gathers the scattered grains of sand to create improbable masses, which we refer to as culture. The wind has not only blown up around us like a hurricane, sweeping away our villages; it has arisen powerfully inside us as well, so much so that we experience it as the guiding principle of the world and of our existence in it. The world around us has become an uninhabitable desert in which the winds of chance perforce pile up dunes. We ourselves welcome chance, and we pile up dunes to gather ourselves in the process. We have become nomads.

⚜ ⚜ ⚜   Now we will try to integrate the two phenomenological perspectives of settledness and nomadism, sitting and wandering, possession and experience, habit and danger, into the Paleolithic Age, Neolithic Age, and the Immediate Future, the three-part division of the span of human existence. The Paleolithic Age poses no problems in this regard. During that time people, from *Homo erectus* and *habilis* through Lascaux and beyond, were typical nomads. They wandered from part-goal to part-goal like weather through a region. They owned nothing and lived neither privately nor politically—they lived in experience. Their life was experience. But problems begin to arise with the Neolithic. Not everyone simply ate their fill patiently, awaiting the maturation of grain to be harvested; some of them followed sheep, goats, and camels on horseback. Not all peoples burned forests to create artificial grassland. Some of them congregated at the edge of the forests, on the remaining steppe. And this division of humankind into the settled and the nomadic was not in the least blunted by bronze and iron. These actually accentuated the division. So, it isn't the case that Neolithic humans were settled: there was a dialectic between settledness and wandering. This needs to be looked at more closely.

If someone had been able to look down on the earth from the moon during the Neolithic, he would have seen only two man-made structures: the Roman *limes* and the Great Wall of China, both of which served to protect the settled from the nomadic. The two are synchronized, although their respective architects knew nothing of each other. Europe became the center of the world because the Great Wall was better constructed than the *limes;* the West was more profoundly impregnated by the nomadic *logos spermaticus* than was the East. The third civilization, India, didn't have to build a wall; it had the Himalayas, to its great detriment.

Why do nomads want to breach civilizations, and why can't the latter civilize them? Because absurdly nomads want to possess [*besitzen*] without settling [*sitzen*]. And because as soon as civilized peoples advance against nomads (whether in the form of military, religious, or research missions), they become possessed by the wind. This is why the dialectic of settledness/wandering could never reach synthesis. Whoever possesses experiences nothing, and whoever experiences possesses nothing.

The Neolithic (8000 B.C. to today) was primarily a time of settledness, initially along swampy river banks and later in ever-higher cement towers with interspersed tin-roof huts. Nevertheless, the nomadic minority always set the tone—not as the more-or-less golden hordes that founded threatening empires in the heartland of humankind (in Central Asia) and at its periphery (in deserts), and forced the majority to reflect on itself, but rather as a whirlwind emanating from the Old Testament, the Koran, and less obviously, Orphic and shamanistic mysteries, infusing the spirit of the majority. These empires and this spirit have certainly run their course. The Turks' siege of Vienna and the murmuring voices of the desert at American universities should be seen as echoes. A probable explanation why this Neolithic dialectic between property and experience has subsided is because it has become too windy to own anything at all. Where there is nothingness (where everything has been calculated down to particles), the emperor, whether he be imperator or khan, loses his justification. The Neolithic Age has come to an end because we have begun to live nomadically. And so, the two phenomenological positions have now been integrated into the three divisions that I proposed, which means that they were justified.

We may now speak of a present breaching catastrophe that will make the world uninhabitable, tear us from our homes, and expose us to danger. The same thing could be stated more optimistically. We have been settled for 10,000 years, perhaps as punishment for a sin that we committed during the transition from the Paleolithic to the Neolithic. The Paleolithic, teeming with easily hunted herbivores and luxuriating in berries and mushrooms, was paradise, and perhaps our original sin consisted in our having settled down in it. But we have served our time and are being released. The catastrophe is that we are now forced to be free. And this explains our emerging interest in nomadism.

❦ ❦ ❦　Nomads*

But first let us look at the etymology of the word *nomad*, because etymology often reveals surprising connections. The word comes from the Greek *nomas*, or "pasture seeker," which in turn comes from *nomos*, which can be translated as "bounded area." The suffix *-nomy*, as in *astronomy* or *autonomy*, is derived from this word. *Astronomy* thus means the bounded area of stars, and *autonomy*, the bounded area of personal decision making. The word *nomos*, in turn, comes from *nemein*, "to grant, to assign." This is the derivation of our word *nemesis*, revenge in the sense of returning something to its just and proper state. The verb *nemein* can be traced back to the ancient Indo-European root *n-m**, which expresses self-subjugation to an order or law (as, for example, in the Sanskrit word *nam*). We derive the word *number* from this root. If we ponder this conceptual context, we can sense what the Greeks meant by the word *nomad*: a person searching for boundaries or limits set for him, for a region or area in which he has legal status. Naturally, this represents how settled people (those who see themselves as having legal status) view wanderers (whom they see as outside the law). This conception surfaces in the way police deal with Gypsies: they are to keep to parking areas set aside for them and are put in their place when they don't (nemesis in police uniform).

　The word *nomad* denotes a person who cannot be defined in terms of place or time, in contrast to the spatial and temporal definability of settled existence. *Defining* itself means "setting boundaries," such as walls. For example, Chinese farmers are spatially and temporally defined by walls, and nomads live beyond those walls. And with this

*This essay is an excerpt from a longer article with the same title, published in Horst Gerhard Haberl, ed., *auf, und, davon: Eine Nomadologie der Neunziger* (Graz: Droschl, 1990).

observation we may successfully conclude our digression into etymology. It allows us to hook into historical considerations remarked on previously.

The ecological catastrophe that forced humans to eat grass seed also forced us to define ourselves, that is, to become settled and to build walls. In this light, our settledness, which has lasted at least 10,000 years, may be seen as a form of imprisonment. We have been sitting in confinement, and now we are being released. This assertion demands that we look more closely at building, dwelling, and according to Heidegger, thinking as well. These ruminations began in the kitchen; now we are forced to look around the kitchen itself and at its walls. We have to make the transition from economics to architecture because, essentially, the hypothesis that asserts that the nineties presage the end of settledness implies that we are being released from architecture. We will no longer con-struct, and all walls will either collapse or be brought down—and not only those in Berlin. We will become undefined and indefinable (but not necessarily infinite and unrestricted). Walls are our subject.

⚑ ⚑ ⚑   If it is true that we have been defined by walls ever since we became settled and that these walls are being perforated, then the question, "What are we?" can no longer be posed in this form. Since the Information Revolution we have become indefinable. We can no longer be localized spatially or temporally. Then again, we might ask under what circumstances, what *Bewandtnis,* it would be possible to speak of ourselves—of an "I"—at all. It sounds complicated, but it really is quite simple. The question has to be posed in terms of cables rather than of walls. A cable is a medium, that is, something that transmits, that forges relationships—it is a channel that allows something to turn toward and relate to something else. Ever since the walls were penetrated, we have ceased to be localizable or definable, but as a result we may for the first time be experienced concretely, because all definition is a form of imprisonment and does not make allowance for concrete experience. Only now that we cannot be labeled, cannot be classified and rubricated, only now that we are no longer settled, can we experience what is essential about ourselves. This means that we can experience ourselves as embedded in a concrete relationship, as the Other of an Other. We are, in effect, the terminal end of a cable.

At first glance it might seem that after the collapse of the walls—the failure of all-defining thought—an unimaginable gaping hole (chaos) opened up to swallow us. As if we (that is, "us," the "we," and the "I") were lost. This is how things appear at first glance after walls have newly caved in; it is the view of a Kafka, a Heidegger, or a Sartre—of any view that gazes into the void. But at the beginning of the nineties we are no longer arrested by first glances; we want a second. We see no longer a void but rather concrete (if transparent) relational fields. The postwar period has taught us not to trust in hard things or in persons even more hardened but to look through them. And in so doing we catch a glimpse of that which is really essential lying behind the apparently objective hardness, namely, the relationship. Television is a good example: we look through the hard box and see the "program." In other words, we see the relationship between the box and the television station. The example of Jacob's tents may illustrate this relational understanding even better.

The roof of a tent does not define up and down the way the roof of a house does. This is because the wind that blows about the tent could knock it over like an umbrella. The wind is a voice that calls out, "Hear!" This collapsible tent roof is like a megaphone; it resonates to the voice. Whoever is hidden within the tent has to hear, but that doesn't mean that he has to obey. He is free to take up the calling or to reject it. "Hear, O Israel," does not necessarily mean, "You must obey." However, whoever takes up the calling enters into a relationship. He was called and is therefore responsible. He now has to answer to the call. A dialogic relationship thus results: an "I" is created because the call addresses a "you." The calling is the concrete experience, and "I" am its consequence.

⚜ ⚜ ⚜   I wish to reiterate the difference between settled people and nomads suggested previously, that the settled possess, whereas nomads experience. What this means will now become clearer. First, of course, there is the external difference, namely, that the settled sit and do not move about, whereas nomads move about and squat (instead of sitting properly). But this external difference is emblematic of an internal one as well. The settled have divided the world and themselves into sections, *nomai,* and concepts on which they sit, and they strive to possess ever more of these sections. And nomads experience concrete networked reality; they move about in it and travel over fields of potentiality. This is not the traditional differentiation made between rationalists and empiricists, such as was made, say, between Anglo-Saxon and Continental philosophy at the time of the Enlightenment. The rift between settled and nomad goes deeper. Nomads consider the possession of concepts to be a form of madness, while the settled see only meaningless drivel in undefined roaming through experience. For example, the nomadic worldview at the core of Judeo-Christianity is mumbo jumbo to those who live a regulated, settled life, though they may be loath to admit it. And this is exactly what seems to be turning around in the nineties.

Viewed externally, walls are collapsing because they are being perforated by cables, but this expresses something internal as well. Rational, conceptual thinking is disintegrating, too, because it is being perforated by calculatory analysis. Both objects and subjects are disintegrating, and nothing remains to be possessed, nor is there anything capable of possessing anymore. Everything is disintegrating into calculated grains of sand, but the relational network, a *mathesis universalis,* is becoming visible behind this desert. That is where experience lies. We are becoming nomads.

❦ ❦ ❦   There can be no doubt that we are leaving our enclosures and moving out into the dust. The objective, physical world is disintegrating into dust, into particles. Life within it is also disintegrating into dust, into genes. Our thinking is disintegrating into dust, into bits of information. Our decisions, into dust, into decidemes. Our actions, into dust, into actemes. And everything about it is getting dusty, such as culture turning into a dust pile of culturemes; language, into a dust pile of phonemes. And we rove ghostlike about the windswept, shifting dunes in this Saharan landscape, like scraps of a previous but now definitively lost rational, conceptual, and scientific understanding. In this sense we are undoubtedly becoming nomadic. But something in this description is not quite right, because after we have laid waste to everything through calculation (granulation, pulverization), we can make it blossom again thanks to computation (assemblage, networking). We can concretize something out of the abstract dust particles (abstract because nondimensional). In other words, we are making our getaway into the dust.

⚜ ⚜ ⚜   If we look at it more closely, we can see how, starting with nothing, we can become something. This may occur as a result of networking. Computing is the concentration of abstract, potential particles out of a networked dispersion. How this occurs may be seen from computer-generated grids in which outpouchings and bends develop at intersections in the grid. The denser the outpouching, the more concretely and the more numerous the potentials that have become realized within it. What at one time was called the "self" or the "I" is just such a realization of potentials, in the same way as is what once was called an "object" or "thing." It is simply that such outpouchings result from a concentration of a networked dispersion. What this means is that potentials gather together to be realized. I am whatever I am because a few dispersed potentials concentrated together. And the more densely they concentrate, the more realized I am. If an anthropology of this sort were ever developed, it would become clear that the confluence of potentials and the collecting of dispersions result in the concrete experience that we label "I" and "you." We are fleeting potentials that approach one another so that we may experience each other as a concrete "I" and a concrete "you." We approach one another for our mutual realization, and (somewhat more concealed) to create an objective world. That is what is meant by a nomadic anthropology, and it implies "computing." But that does not mean that the Neolithic Age, with its possessive and possessed rationality, its imprisonment within four walls, and its pizza sliced into sections, has been overcome. A further step in the direction of "posthistory" is needed.

The settled person, the farmer, and the citizen can be localized in space; they have defining addresses. That disintegrates as soon as we compute. Within the network everyone is an omnipresent potential. But a geographical definition requires a historical definition, and the address requires a date. Not only does the settled person possess territory; he also possesses a slice of time, a duration. The ability to cut a section out of time, and the transformation of time into a pizza with sections (called years, hours, or seconds), requires that he see time as both uniform and irreversible. A clock must tick away at the same constant speed and never run backward. Such a conception of time is known as "historical consciousness." This is the consciousness of the Neolithic Age, even though it came to predominate only with the invention of linear script, during the Bronze Age.

This type of historical time, however, cannot be experienced. We do not experience all seconds as being equally long, whether we are in the dentist's chair or having an orgasm. We do not experience time as if it could not be reversed, say, in flashbacks. And above all, we do not experience time as emanating from the past, which is what clock time requires. Concrete experience demonstrates that (as the word implies) the future arrives.* The settled person has a clear and distinct concept of historical time, but one that falsifies the concrete experience of time. Only after we have broken out of our walls, which tag us with the three coordinates of address and the coordinate of date, will we be able to experience time again.

We are in the process of learning that with some difficulty. Words like *synchronicity* and *retrieve* are symptomatic of this learning process. They imply that time is a potential from which we may compute concrete things that can be experienced. So-called events can be observed and stored everywhere simultaneously and can be retrieved from storage for the purpose of computation. This means that only the present (that is, existence and storage) is concrete and that the past and the future are interchangeable potential forms of time. If such a consciousness were actually elaborated—and we are far from achieving that—we would then be able to speak of a posthistorical consciousness.

It may well be that the Paleolithic nomadic hunter-gatherers and perhaps even the Neolithic nomadic herders live until this day with a

---

Zukunft ("future") is made up of *zu-* and *kommen;* that is, it "comes toward" or approaches (consider also *Ankunft*). Although we say things such as "As the time approaches," this sense is not accessible in the English word *future,* which is derived from the Latin *esse,* "to be."

prehistoric, mythic, and cyclical consciousness of time.* By this I mean that for them everything repeats and that in this eternal return of sameness they live their wandering, their back and forth—that they live experience. That will surely not be the case with us. We will have storage in the form of memory. But like our nomadic forebears, we will not *make* history (because we won't have a future); rather, we will *have* history. To some extent we will stand above history and reach into it and intervene from above. For this reason, however, we will not take an inter-est in it. Only then will we have superseded the Neolithic.

This form of nomadism is one in which dispersed potentials approach each other via a networked structure so that they may experience a mutual "I" and "you" and dialogue *above* history. Such nomadism, which constantly realizes itself concretely, can no longer be understood using the categories of the Neolithic. It is not about possession (economics) or the public (politics); nor is it about reality or fiction, theory or praxis. Other categories will have to be worked out, and their contours are already discernible. The rational, causal, and definitional way of thinking will yield to a thought field that is relational and probabilistic. In all likelihood our current language will no longer be able to articulate these categories. We will have to avail ourselves of other codes, perhaps computer codes. To the extent that we can see beyond the nineties, it seems that aesthetic criteria will supplant our present ethical and epistemological ones. The nomad who emerges from the nineties will more likely be an artist than a hunter or herdsman. Out of dispersed potentials he will artfully compute concrete realities (effects rather than realities). As in the Paleolithic, he will still be *Homo faber,*† but more consciously so. Unlike his forebears, who manufac-

---

*In the first part of this essay, Flusser designates the nineties as the end of the Neolithic Age and of human settledness; the nineties mark a change in human existence from life as settled farmers or grain eaters to that as nomadic shepherds, or "*Er-fahrer.*" According to Flusser, the settled farmers accumulated hardware (property) and software (the alphanumeric code), which provided them with a history and a memory. Nomadic shepherds, in turn, did not construct a memory since they "*er-fahren*" history without storing it. Now this transient state of settledness is about to end. With new "artificial and efficient memories," Flusser claims, the nomads of the nineties will present the exact opposite of the historical nomads in that they will "possess history without making history."

†Latin: "man the maker."

tured chisels that simulated readily available incisors, he will experience both incisor and chisel as having the same ontological standing—as computations of potentials. The nineties will lead the way out of the Neolithic Age but not back into the Paleolithic. It will lead us into open territory as yet unexplored, into unrealized potentials.

⚜ ⚜ ⚜ Building Houses

We are animals that dwell, whether in nests, caves, tents, houses, cubes stacked one atop another, mobile homes, or under bridges. Because without a habitual place to live, we would experience nothing. It is not necessary to know anything about information theory to arrive at this insight. Being a tourist is sufficient. Experience is noise that gains meaning only in the habitual, that is, is therein transformed into information. There can be no such thing as a tourist without lodging; otherwise he would stumble about in chaos and not experience anything. The Middle Ages conceived of humans as homeless tourists, as *homines viatores,* a footloose mob adrift in a vale of woes. Moses Maimonides wrote his *Guide for the Perplexed* at this time. Now we use Michelin guides, and we often still have trouble finding the way home.

Signs of a new homelessness are beginning to accumulate. This is probably because our homes are no longer up to the task of processing noise into experience. We will probably have to reconfigure our houses. Houses consist of a roof, walls with windows, and doors as well as of miscellaneous less important components. The roof is the crucial element: *roofless* and *homeless* are synonymous. Roofs are tools of subordinate subjects, who can duck under them and hide from their masters (whether God or nature). The German word for "roof" (*Dach*) has the same root as the Greek *techne:* roofers are thus the true artists. They create the line of demarcation between what is the prerogative of the sovereign and what is the private sphere of the abject subject. What happens under a roof comes under only limited legal jurisdiction. Even hominids used tree canopies as roofs for their nests. But we no longer believe in transcendent or natural laws that are imposed on us; rather, we imagine that we ourselves project the laws. We have no further need of roofs.

❦ ❦ ❦   Walls are defensive structures against threats from outside, not from above. The word *Mauer* comes from the Latin *munire* ("to protect"). They are a form of munitions. There are actually two walls: the external wall is turned toward dangerous aliens and potential immigrants (coming from the outside); the internal wall is turned toward the inmates of the house to guarantee their safety. This function is clear in walls that do not define homes (such as the Berlin Wall or the Great Wall of China). The external wall is political; the internal wall, secret; and the function of the wall as a whole is to protect the secret from the sinister and uncanny. Whoever despises secrecy must tear down walls.

But even petty secretizers and patriots have to cut holes—windows and doors—into walls to exit and enter and to peer out. Before the German word *Schau* became synonymous with the English *show*, it described that inside-looking-out whose instrument was the window. One could peer outside without becoming wet. The Greeks called that *theoria*. Knowledge without danger or direct experience. Today we can poke instruments out the window and gain experience without being endangered. The epistemological question is this: are experiments inappropriate to the extent to which they are carried out through a window (from theory)? Or is it necessary to walk out through the door to gain hands-on (phenomenological) experience? Windows are no longer reliable instruments.

❦ ❦ ❦   Doors are our exit and entrance holes in walls. We go outside to experience the world and to lose ourselves in it, and then we return home to find ourselves again—and in the process we lose the world that we had wanted to conquer. This movement in and out is what Hegel referred to as "unhappy consciousness."* We can even return home to find the door locked. True, we carry our keys in our pockets, that is, we can decode the secret password, but that password might have been changed while we were out. Insidiousness [*Heimtücke*] is characteristic of home

---

*Georg Wilhelm Friedrich Hegel writes on "unhappy consciousness in "Freiheit des Selbstbewußtseins; Stoizismus, Skeptizismus, und das unglückliche Bewußtsein," *Phänomenologie des Geistes* (*Phenomenology of Spirit*) (1807), chap. 4 (B).

and heimat. When that happens, we are left under the rain spout without a roof. Doors are neither felicitous nor reliable instruments.

The following objections may also be made against windows and doors. People can look into and climb through windows, and what is public can break and enter the privacy of the home through the door. Of course, we can fortify our windows against spies and thieves by installing iron bars, and a drawbridge will keep the police from our door, but then we would live in fear and constriction within our four walls. Architects with this in mind don't have much of a future.

Roofs, walls, windows, and doors are no longer functional in the present, and this explains why we are beginning to feel so un-at-home. But since we cannot easily return to tents and caves (although some people try), we must, for better or worse, design new types of houses.

❦ ❦ ❦   And in fact a start has been made in this direction. The perfect house with a roof, walls, windows, and doors exists only in fairy tales. Material and nonmaterial cables have perforated it, making it like Swiss cheese. The roof sports an antenna, telephone wires pierce the walls, windows are replaced by television, and doors have given way to garage and automobile. The perfect house has become a ruin through whose cracks gust the winds of communication. It has become a shabby patchwork. A new type of architecture is needed.

Architects must now stop thinking geographically and begin to conceptualize topologically. A house should be conceived of no longer as an artificial cave but rather as a bending in the field of interpersonal relations. It won't be easy to transform our thinking. It was accomplishment enough to transform geographical thinking from the planar to the spherical. But topographical thinking may be facilitated by computer-generated images of equations. In these images the earth is no longer envisaged merely as a geographical place in the solar system; it may instead be viewed as a bending in the gravitational field of the sun. This is how we must envision the house: as a bending in the field of interpersonal relations to which relationships are attracted as to a magnet. An attractive house of this sort would gather relationships, process them into information, store the information, and then forward or redirect it to others. A creative house would be a node in the network of interpersonal relations.

⚘ ⚘ ⚘   But such a house constructed of cabling would be full of dangers. For example, instead of being used for networking, the cables could become bundled—"fascistic" rather than "dialogic." Like television rather than like the telephone. In this horrific scenario houses would become the prop of an unimaginable totalitarianism. Architects must ensure reversibility of the network wiring. That is a technical task to which architects are equal.

Nevertheless, this sort of housing construction represents a technological revolution that goes beyond the current competence of architecture. (This, incidentally, pertains to all technological revolutions.) Such architecture without roofs or walls, which would be open to all the world—in other words, would consist only of reversible windows and doors—would change our existence. People would no longer be able to duck and hide, and they would have neither foundation nor support. They would have no choice but to extend a hand to others. They would no longer be subjects. There would be no masters from whom they had to hide, but neither would they be able to seek their protection. And there would be no nature to threaten them or that they would feel the need to tame. On the other hand, these mutually open houses would spawn an unimaginable abundance of projects. They would be networklike switched projectors for alternative worlds that all humankind would hold in common.

Housing construction of this sort would be a dangerous adventure. But it would be less dangerous than staying stuck in the ruins we are currently inhabiting. The upheaval that we are witnessing forces us to hazard the undertaking. If it succeeds, which is not out of the question, we would once again be able to dwell, be able to process noise into information—be able to experience. If we do not take up the challenge, we will forever be condemned to squat in front of the television between four perforated walls, under a perforated roof, or to roam about aimlessly in our automobiles gathering no experience at all.

✿ ✿ ✿ "How Goodly Are Your Tents, Jacob"

Our conference here in Graz* deals with the issue of whether we are in the process of losing the roofs over our heads. The answer depends on our definition of the concept "roof." As people who have heretofore had housing, we tend to the view that a roof is something that is propped up by walls. And when we speak of walls, we mean solid structures, because we cannot imagine a roof supported by canvas. Given such definitions of *wall* and *roof*, we can actually count on ever higher levels of homelessness, for we are everywhere tearing down walls, either because they impede traffic or because they get in the way of the free flow of people, goods, or information. Roofs supported by solid walls don't have much of a future. However, such a limited meaning of *roof* is itself a consequence of the limiting quality of walls. Once solid walls have fallen, we will be more likely to think "canvas" when we speak of roof and wall. Within this expanded sense of the word, there is no room for homelessness. This expanded sense, however, will require that architects transform their ways of thinking. They will have to think more in terms of tents than houses.

This essay will also examine tents, but not from a primarily architectonic perspective. Its author lacks the necessary competence, but he hopes nonetheless that his remarks will contain some kernels that will be of use to architects. He will try to examine tents without preconception (phenomenologically, as they say) to get at their essence. The difficulty is that we have so little experience with tents compared to our experience with houses. One might think that this would be more

*This paper was presented at the annual Steirischer Herbst, an avant-garde literary and art festival, in Graz, Austria, October 1990 (theme: "Mobile Hall").

of an advantage than a disadvantage. After all, we currently spend most of our time in houses, and so we have no distance from them. They are shrouded in habit, and each of us harbors a raft of preconceptions about them. This is the problem that architects face: they are dealing with such a commonplace and ordinary thing that is surrounded by so many preconceptions that they must first develop a definition of what is essential to a house. It seems that it is easier to access what is essential to tents than what is essential to houses, and it seems that architects could approach tents more creatively. That, however, would be an error. Tents are shrouded in an ideological fog precisely because we have relatively so little experience with them—romantic ideas about camping tents are one example. My task here will be to bracket out such preconceptions without forgoing their connotations (especially biblical ones).

The essential thing about a tent is that one puts it up, finds shelter under it, and then folds it up again. This formulation of the essence of tents brings umbrellas immediately to mind. And in fact the umbrella is the form of tent with which we have the greatest experience. But to really get at the essence of tents, we need to think about devices such as parachutes and television screens and not just umbrellas and parasols. Be that as it may, what is immediately apparent is that architects have neglected tents. There are a lot of stupid contraptions, but umbrellas are among the most absurd. For example, umbrellas are relatively complicated devices that fail at precisely the moment they are needed most, such as when it is windy. They afford only minimal protection, are inconvenient to carry, and actually pose a malicious danger to other people's eyes—and people lose and switch umbrellas all the time. True, there have been a variety of umbrella styles, but actually there has been no technical progress since the ancient Egyptians, and when people say, "God Eternal is my protector" [*Schirm* = "umbrella"],* it verges on blasphemy.

When you watch how quickly and easily huge circus tents are erected and then pulled down and folded up again, you might be tempted to

*Flusser is most likely referring to Psalm 91 in Luther's 1545 translation of the Bible: "Seine Wahrheit ist Schirm und Schild" (Ps. 91:4).

think that umbrellas really aren't that bad. It isn't their fault that people have so much trouble with them, but they will learn as soon as they begin to tent. But as soon as you consider parachutes, you once again see how absurd umbrellas are. People jump out of an airplane, and the wind automatically unfolds the device. It is only after one is on the ground that one is faced with the difficult task of refolding. Parachutes make us realize what is so infuriatingly inane about umbrellas—and about tents in general (assuming that the umbrella is the essence of tent). Since the time of the Egyptians, neither architects nor tent designers in general have recognized that they are dealing with wind, not just with gravity. They have not considered that what is dangerous about umbrellas and tents is not that they may collapse but that they can be picked up and blown away by the wind. That will change. We will learn to think more "nonmaterially" once the walls have been torn down.

Let us once again try to capture in words the essence of tents. They are an umbrella-like shelter that is unfolded and set up in the wind, is used for protection from the wind, and is taken down and folded up again in the wind. And of course that formulation immediately brings to mind sails. And in fact sails are that form of tent that uses the wind to the fullest. The tent as umbrella tries to withstand the wind; the tent as sail, however, tries to exploit the power of the wind. The sail is as clever a device as the umbrella is absurd. A well-built sailboat can sail virtually against the wind and is powerless only when the wind stands still. And a glider can ply its way both horizontally and vertically on the wind. And so architects of the future will have to consider kites, such as those that children make dance in the wind, as well as umbrellas as they design living spaces.

The recognition of the essence of tents allows us to see parachutes and gliders as two variations among many on a "tent" theme because we can now recognize the tent as a canvas construction that billows in the wind. Canvas in contrast to solid wall; billowing in the wind in contrast to breaking the wind. This is not the worst place to begin an analysis of the cultural change that is breaking on us. Before we examine the wall problem in greater depth, however, we must first consider the wind, which brings us back to ancient domains. Namely, although we can hear the wind (it may roar deafeningly) and may feel it (it can knock us over), what we can see is never the wind but only its disastrous consequences. What I have just said also applies to spirits and ghosts, to gods and to God the Creator. All these words are derived from our experience of the wind. This is attested to in the Hebrew, Greek, and Latin words for wind (and for the movement of air generally)—*ruach, pneuma,* and *spiritus*—and in their traditions they also denote the holy spirit. As soon as we move from solid walls to canvas ones, it seems that we are entering the kingdom of the spirit, or to express it less theologically, everything becomes more nonmaterial.

And now on to the walls that billow in the wind. A tent wall is a wind wall, whether it is rammed into the ground like a circus tent, is stretched out on a stick like an umbrella, floats in the air like a parachute or kite, or swells on the mast like a sail. By contrast, a solid wall is a rock face, regardless of its actual composition or the number of doors and windows it has. Because of this a house is like a cave in the rock, from which it is actually derived, a dark, mysterious secret [*Geheimnis*]—a "refuge" [*Heim*]. And a tent is like a tree nest, whose descendant it is—a place of gathering and diverging, a place of calm in the wind. We possess in houses; they are themselves possessions, and this possession is defined by walls. We wander into a tent; it gathers up experience, and this experience branches and ramifies through the tent wall. That the tent wall is a network, a membrane, and that this network processes experience is contained in the German word *Leinwand** itself. It is a textile that is open to experience (open to the wind and spirit) and then stores these experiences. And then again, since time immemorial, the tent wall has stored images in the form of carpets; since the invention of oil paints, canvas has stored paintings on walls; since the invention of film, it has stored moving pictures; since the invention of television, it has served as a screen for electromagnetically produced images; and since the invention of computer plotters,† it has allowed the now nonmaterial tent wall to branch and ramify images,

---

*The German word *Leinwand* means both "linen" and "canvas." The *-wand* in *Leinwand* means "wall," thus a "wall of canvas."

†Plotters are used for precision drawing and printing (e.g., in engineering). They differ from standard printers in that they use pens to draw lines.

thanks to the processing that takes place in its membrane. The tent wall, billowing in the wind, gathers experiences, processes them, and then passes them on. It is because of its wall that the tent is such a nest of creativity.

The image of the tent that I have just offered up, as a sort of nest enclosed by wind walls that gathers, processes, and transmits information through channels that branch within it, is both a utopian and an archaic one. It is archaic inasmuch as the nestlike tents that were built under the tree canopy and protected our prehuman ancestors from danger must have worked this way. And it is utopian because this is how one might imagine the telematic society, in which both material and nonmaterial wires will become knotted into tentlike collection hubs. But this overview may offer the architect new ways of looking at our imminent houseless future precisely because this perspective on the tent links what is archaic and what is utopian and because it appears to ignore canvas, hide, and rag tents that form the border between them.

And yet, this essay cannot simply neglect the tents that are located between the prehuman and the posthuman. I will therefore mention two extreme forms of tents, Genghis Khan's yurts and Jacob's tents. When the time comes for walls to be torn down, architects will have two models to emulate: Genghis Khan's mobile halls and Jacob's tents. Everything seems to point in the direction of mobile halls, but we shouldn't give up on Jacob's tents.

The enormous yurt of this conqueror of the world, whose empire stretched from the Baltic to the Sea of Japan, and from the Arctic to the Indian Ocean, was covered with colorful streamers. These streamers, which waved in the wind, and the wind bells that were affixed to the yurt formed the actual tent wall. Whenever a foreigner crossed the steppe and approached Genghis Khan's tent to lay his experience at the conqueror's feet, he would see the fluttering streamers a whole day's journey off. We are familiar with streamers of this sort from modern Turkistan but also from the banners of the National Socialists. They are shamanistic devices that implore the spirits to serve the will of the ruler. These winds blow around the tent so that it may ride on the wind, so that it may become an air castle. Genghis Khan's yurt was a sailing vessel that rose up on the seething waves of wind to conquer heaven. And all spirits, both good and bad, flapped and tacked to create a mobile hall out of fluttering streamers.

The unassuming tents of Jacob, on the other hand, seem to evade the hot wind of the steppe. But in fact this evasion is a form of hearkening. Balaam's donkey, as we know, brayed out, "How goodly are your tents, Jacob," although he initially intended to scold him. Observant Jews repeat this sentence whenever they enter the synagogue. It probably occasioned much Talmudic disputation from all sides. But here I will ask only what the donkey meant by *goodly*. Those tents were certainly nothing like Genghis Khan's magnificent yurt. They were not hung with carpets or decorated with enormous streamers. Nor did they rise from the landscape like palaces. The donkey must have had something else in mind—perhaps the experience that tent dwellers (including himself, Balaam, and Jacob) have of desert and steppe winds. A tent is supposed to afford protection from the wind, and it billows. For the tent dweller it must act as an amplifier of the wind's voice. The tent dweller cannot help but hear that voice. The voice calls out to him. But he doesn't necessarily have to obey. "Hear, O Israel," does not necessarily mean "follow." (*Israel* is Jacob's honorific.) But if he follows nonetheless, then the call of the wind becomes his calling. He then accepts the responsibility for answering that call. Jacob's tents were "goodly" because he answered the call of the wind, because he accepted the responsibility. The wall of Jacob's tent is the membrane that allows him to hear the fantastic and through which he accepts responsibility in answer to that call. Theologians have for thousands of years argued over the precise message that the steppe wind utters through the tent wall, thereby transforming the tent into a medium of the fantastic. Perhaps it utters nothing more than "I am that I am," challenging Jacob to become what he should be. But whatever the message mediated by the tent wall may be, it is the message that underpins our culture.

❦ ❦ ❦ Ex-perience

All ideologies of progress proceed from the assumption that we are moving forward. This much is obvious: we have two eyes that point forward, and our legs take us in that same direction. We are beings that want to follow our noses. Or put another way: we go to meet our death, and on the way we encounter obstacles that we either deal with, leap over, or avoid. This encounter between ourselves and things is what we call experience [*Er-fahrung*].* But anyone who takes a closer look will recognize that this conception is not correct and that progress is somehow lacking. If we were to record our steps on a flat surface, we would see that we are not moving forward so much as oscillating back and forth. That our path through life consists primarily of movement out the door and then a return home through the door. Put another way: we go out into the world to experience, and we lose ourselves in the process; we then return home to find ourselves again, and we lose the world that we experienced. In other words, we don't follow our noses but rather move in and out, and our path through life is not one of progress but one of swarming. The model we are patterned on is not so much the lone coyote who follows his prey to experience it but rather the anthill.

If we relinquish this conception of our path through life and entertain a different one, the word *experience* acquires another, deeper meaning. To do this, we must imagine that we are not moving from the present into the future. Doing so is an existential impossibility, because wherever we are, we are in the present. We cannot escape the present without having relinquished ourselves. To the contrary, the fu-

*Flusser hyphenates the German word *Erfahrung* (*Er-fahrung*) to accentuate the two components of the word. *Er-* is a particle that denotes an action into or out of and about, toward an end; *fahren* means "to drive or go," "to fare."

ture comes to meet us in our present, and this is precisely what is implied in the German word *Zukunft*.* We are always in the here and now, and the future advances toward us in our here and now from all directions. (This should be obvious; however, the ideology of progress, with its insane concept of time advancing toward us from the past, has blinded us.) Our path through life is not a forward movement but rather a path of time moving in our direction, and experience is not something that we come on but something that happens to us. It is not active but passive; not so much a deed or act as something we suffer. We experience the world not because we move out into it but because it approaches us.† This is something we need to keep in mind here.

In spite of the complexity of our nervous system, neurophysiology is beginning to gain insight into the process of experience. To summarize the current state of knowledge: pointlike elements continually stream toward our neurons from all directions. Once these elements have reached a certain threshold of intensity, they are perceived as stimuli, and this perception is digitally encoded. The response is all or nothing; there are no strong or weak stimuli. The received stimuli are then processed by the nervous system in ways that are not yet clear, resulting in notions, feelings, wishes, and thoughts; in short, this is how we experience. Drawing on a computer model, we may speak of a computation of experience generated from digital code. Or put another way: experience is how the nervous system actualizes incoming virtualities.

I was being somewhat cagey in sketching out this brief introduction to the neurophysiological basis of experience. I wanted to show that thought and body are two extrapolations from the concrete process of experience and that they cannot be understood in isolation from each other. One can also express the idea like this: experience is a concrete relationship, one of the relationships out of which our concept of life in the world is built. Both that which is experienced and that which experiences may be extrapolated from this concrete relationship, and

---

*See the footnote on p. 52.

†*Angehen* has several meanings in German, among them (1) "to approach" and (2) "to concern." That is, the world approaches us, and we experience it because it concerns us.

in turn, body and thought may be extrapolated from that which experiences. What is crucial in this rather cumbersome formulation
(taken from Husserl's phenomenology) is that there can be no experience of the body without the experience of thought—and no thought
without the experience of the body. There are several other aspects of
this formulation that require further consideration.

Let us imagine that our central nervous system were to extend
around the globe like a net. Let us further imagine that it would constitute something like a *neurosphere* situated between the biosphere
and the atmosphere. What I am suggesting is not science fiction but
the model on which the telematic society now being built is based.*
What we need to do is imagine such a neurosphere as a network of
human nerves as well as material and nonmaterial cables. And we must
further imagine human brains and artificial intelligences at the nodal
intersections of such a network. Such a neurosphere spanning the
globe would function to compute into experience all stimuli inces-
santly streaming in from all directions and to transform these experiences into decisions and actions. Seen this way, the telematic society
would be a mechanism for experience, a global machine for the realization of potentials. In this perspective, neither body (in this case the
globe) nor thoughts (in this case the information transmitted across
the wires of the network) would be mobile in the process of experience. The only part of that process that would be mobile would be the
incoming virtualities. This had to be brought up because in the concrete, lived process of experience, not only do stimuli stream toward
us, but we ourselves turn toward them, for example, with our eyes or
hands. What we must bear in mind is that in principle experiences re-

---

Telematic is an essential term in Flusser's thinking. It combines the prefix *tele-*, which in
Flusser's notion connotes proximity and closeness, with automation, or as Flusser puts it,
"humans' liberation from everything that can be mechanized" (see "Die Welt ist unsäglich
aber zählbar: Vilém Flusser über Telematik, technische Bilder und das reine nulldimension-
ale Denken," in Thomas Mießgang, *X-Sample: Gespräche am Rande der Zeit* [Vienna: Passagen, 1993], 25–50). The telematic society underscores yet again Flusser's argument for a dialogic principle in today's high-speed and global environment. As such, it is a deeply
egalitarian concept that presumes a network of humans and machines (society) ready to exchange and synthesize information to create dialogue and discourse without the censoring
powers inherent to a center, headquarters, or directive.

quire neither bodily nor thinking movement. We experience even when totally at rest, and in fact mystics teach that it is at precisely these moments that we experience most powerfully.

Nevertheless, it is not simply the case that what we experience always streams in on us. In fact, we often go out and gather in what there is to experience—go looking for it. This ambiguity is expressed in Latin or the Latin parts of languages. For example, the English word *experience* connotes more what streams toward us, whereas *experiment* connotes what we seek out. Latinate terms dealing with these matters are generally better than their German equivalents. In German the word *er-fahren* means to go until one arrives somewhere. *Ex-periri*, on the other hand, connotes that one has completely exploited or exhausted something. In German we experience a lemon after we have moved about until we bump into it. In Latin we experience it only after we have completely squeezed it out. The formulation from Husserl's phenomenology that I discussed before points to the pathway from German into Latin.

For as long as we thought progressively (i.e., historically), the object was to gather one experience after another. That is a linear, Don Juan sort of way of living: experiencing one woman after another, and 1,003 in Spain alone. Since we have had to give up our historical, linear, progressive consciousness (for reasons I won't go into here), we no longer believe that this arraying of experiences is a good method for experiencing anything. Now we tend to the opinion that it is better to chew away at a single experience until we have completely exhausted it. We now tend to believe that the experience of a man who engages with a single woman has a deeper understanding of women than Don Juan ever could have, even if he had been able to extend his list into infinity. This new antihistorical belief is particularly evident in photography. The camera is a machine created for *ex-periri*. It jumps around the thing to be experienced so that it can experience it from as many different angles as possible. The camera's posthistorical mobility (regardless of whether we call it a thought incarnated or a body ideated) exemplifies the mobility of experience that we are inquiring into here: a dance around a possibility to actualize it.

At this point I want to register a misgiving. As long as we attempted to gather one experience after the other, we were struck by the impossibility of experiencing all that was possible. True, the further we went, the larger became our island of experience. But this island was surrounded by an ocean that could never be experienced, and compared to the ocean, our island was despairingly tiny, even somewhat contemptible. To put it another way: back then we could not experience the world because we could not go out into it far enough to explore it completely. The fault lay in us, the explorers, not in the nature of things themselves. Now that we are trying to concentrate on a few tiny experiences that concern us intimately, now that we are no longer going out to explore but rather seek to experience to the fullest all that streams toward us and concerns us, we encounter the opposite limitation. Each concrete experience is surrounded by an infinite swarm of perspectives, and we simply cannot experience any one of them fully, no matter how many perspectives we try to see it from. For example, we can photograph a human face from a thousand angles, light it in a thousand different ways, and even turn the camera and the face itself in a thousand directions, but we still won't even have begun to nibble at the number of possibilities for experiencing it. In other words, the fault is not ours alone or that of our inability to experience the world (as was the case with historical consciousness); rather, the fault lies in the concrete relationship that we have with the world.

The import of this misgiving is that by giving up our progressive consciousness we have made a transition to a different disposition toward experience. Back then we believed that everything could be experienced objectively; the problem was only that we lacked the subjective ability to go everywhere. That position represented a sort of optimism. While it is true that we cannot experience everything, we can experience more and more. Currently we believe that nothing can be completely experienced, and that no matter how long, broad, deep, or high we look, we can never get at the core of any experience. That is a peculiar sort of pessimism. Everything that surrounds us—and we ourselves—is bathed in an unfathomable mystery, and we are able to experience only those aspects of the mystery that approach us, concern us.

Ever since we have learned to think phenomenologically instead of historically, experience has become something that approaches and concerns us. It is a passion and a suffering. But we can open ourselves to this passion, decide to experience. Most people close up because they fear all suffering, and they thus experience little over the courses of their lives. Hardly a future comes to rest in the here and now that such people occupy. A very few of us are prepared to open ourselves to the future and to decide to experience. The mobility in this decision is our preparedness not to take a particular position vis-à-vis any experience that comes our way but rather to try out all possible points of view. The mobility of the body in this decision is to open itself up to experience from all possible sides in order to consider them from those positions. And the mobility of thought is to move the body or instrument back and forth in relation to each experience.

❧ ❧ ❧ Reunification or Networking?

The two Germanies that now exist seem to be contemplating reunification.* Although this event would generally be hailed as a tearing down of walls and borders, it might just be an optical illusion. The opposite could well be true—it could be about defining what is "German" and about erecting borders. Its main feature could be nationalism. A German-speaking land or country is a region in which people avail themselves of a code called standard German for much of their communications. It is a code that was worked out in the process of a previous reunification of various German lands in Karl IV's chancellery in Prague.† The intent was to reduce to a common denominator the diversity of German dialects, say, those spoken in Luxembourg and Bohemia. Reunification is a characteristic that is inherent in standard German. It was supposed to reconstruct, at least on paper, a mythical German that had split into countless dialects. One Germany is a country in which the German typewriter clatters, not the German tongue.

However, standard German is in the process of losing its significance, as is the alphabetic code in general. People increasingly get their information from images and less and less from text. And these images are increasingly computer generated—synthetic images. They are based on digital codes, and the people who manipulate these codes are

---

*This essay first appeared in *Basler Zeitung*, April 10, 1990, five months after the fall of the Berlin Wall, on November 9, 1989, and around six months before the former German Democratic Republic became part of the Federal Republic of Germany on October 3, 1990.

†Although the chancellery of Karl IV was among the first to seek a unified written German language, an official code of *"Schriftdeutsch"* continued to evade scholars and writers until the end of the nineteenth century. A common orthography and pronunciation came about only after 1871, Germany's first unification; in 1901 Austria and Switzerland adopted this standardized form of *Neuhochdeutsch* (new high German).

called "hackers," perhaps because they hack linear codes such as German into the digits 0 and 1. But this name has much more interesting implications as well. It may turn out that hackers will hack to bits all the efforts of the reunifiers.

The difference between digital codes and ones such as standard German is not that they are in some way less "natural," that is, contrived. After all, standard German is a contrived language created with imperial intent. Digital codes differ from standard German in the following ways:

1. Their users choose them freely, whereas the use of standard German is enforced in the schools.
2. They require a networked apparatus (have a dialogic quality), whereas standard German leads to a bundling of relationships (has a discursive quality).
3. Digital codes lead to calculatory, computational, and relational ways of thinking and acting, whereas standard German promotes a more processual, definitional way of existing. These are the differences that will be most crucial for the future.

⚐ ⚐ ⚐   There are signs that "digital" thinking is emerging out of the "linear." This changeover may be observed as a breaking apart of large units into their component parts, which can then be networked together. It is as if a muscle cramp were dissolving. And it can either be viewed as a deliverance [*Erlösung*] or a dissolution [*Auflösung*]. Such uncramping can be observed in numerous arenas: in the loosening of family bonds, in the increasing blurring of class distinctions, in the crumbling of centralized disciplines (in military, church, and even communist parties), and in the melting together of discrete subjects in the universities into interdisciplinary fields of research. Wherever we look we see the dissolution of defined agglomerations in favor of gray zones that can be networked.

However, the example I began with has to do with pan-Europeanism, which entails the abolishment of borders but not the creation of a reunified Europe as attempted by Constantine and Charlemagne. The point is to do the opposite, namely, to break Europe down into its component parts and then to network these parts by means of crisscrossing connections. States of spasm as exemplified by France, Spain, and Italy must be dissolved to facilitate complex networks between such regions as Provence, Catalonia, and Tuscany. The guiding principle is that nationalism, this invention of the enlightened seventeenth- and eighteenth-century bourgeoisie, has proved to be a catastrophic crime and that when giant nation-states are abolished, people will be able to enter into freely chosen associations. These might include work and leisure-time communities instead of national communities. As Goethe put it, relationships of choice rather than of blood.*

❦ ❦ ❦ Unfortunately, people who stroll through the reopened Brandenburg Gate are not in step with pan-Europeanism. The Berlin Wall was torn down not to abolish national borders but to erect them. The point was not to network, say, Brandenburg with Auvergne or Swabia with Wales but to aggregate two Germanies into a unit. And once completed, why not other German-speaking countries? The intent is to promote unity, and this is precisely what pan-Europeanism (and digital thinking in general) seek to prevent. It promotes diversity, not unity, a dispersed network, not reunification.

Hackers are ensconced in front of their networked computers in both these Germanies. By virtue of their sitting there, they are integrated into a global network that connects them with other people across any and all borders. They experience the continual creation of new permutations that are made possible by the strands of this network. They are living proof of the utter wrongheadedness of drawn borders and of the creative power of such gray zones. Might the example of the hacker suffice to cause us to hack at the aggregating, cramped predisposition of the reunifiers? Would it be enough to prevent a Karl IV, Charlemagne, or Constantine from coming to power and to ensure the creation of a dialogically networked, and therefore freer, society? A person looking at the current scene from the outside

*Johann Wolfgang von Goethe, *Die Wahlverwandtschaften: Ein Roman,* pts. 1–2 (Tübingen: Cotta, 1809); published in English as *Elective Affinities.*

would find this improbable. However, those who are aware that the code that produced standard German is nearing exhaustion (the same applies to all forms of nationalism as well), and those who are aware of the creative potential of the new code, will probably be inclined to bet on the hackers and not on the reunifiers.

❦ ❦ ❦   Does the French Nation Still Exist?

This essay was written at a particular moment in history.* The Union of Socialist Council Republics [USSR] is in the process of collapse. This is shocking for two reasons. First of all, council republics are structures whose purpose it is to replace other structures that have become untenable. Second, according to posthistorical analysis there aren't supposed to be any more historical moments. The following essay will examine these two complementary shocks. The use of the expression "French nation" in my title stands in for what have ostensibly become untenable social structures and for an ostensibly superseded history.

People who only a few years ago tried to assess the social situation, particularly in Europe, were struck by the degradation of most traditional structures. Nation, class, family, and marriage, but also less formalized relationships such as master and student or interest groups, seemed to be in a more or less advanced state of decay, to the point where they were polluting the air. On the other hand, no new forms of interpersonal attachment could be discerned emanating from the bubbling stew of the consumer culture. True, the masses, relieved of their received attachments, began to gather at meeting places that exerted a novel attraction, such as television sets, beaches in the summer, ski resorts in the winter, or at various sporadic "events," as they are called. But it was simply not possible to discern, from these structures spun out by the masses, which of them would be able to bear the load of the emotional, intellectual, and aesthetic content of the decaying attachments. Because of this the following prognosis was made at the time:

*This essay first appeared in the weekly *Freitag,* November 15, 1991. Vilém Flusser had presented the paper about ten days earlier, on November 4, 1991, at the Institut Français, the French Cultural Institute, in Berlin.

thanks particularly to the communications revolution, we are entering an amorphous, stewlike state of massification. At the time it appeared that the role of the intellectual would consist, among other things, in discovering, even inventing, alternative intersubjective attachments that would restore a sense of meaning to a life that had become absurd.

❦ ❦ ❦   A short digression is in order at this point. All social structures in the Western tradition may be explained historically as products of culture, but to those who live their lives at the time, these structures appear to be outside history, to be natural phenomena that have always existed in that form. For example, it looks as though marriage, the institution that regulates the life that a man and a woman live together, is at the very least the natural structure for human beings. Pointing out the relatively recent origins of marriage elicits from so-called moral people not merely indignation but a characteristic unwillingness even to entertain the notion. Try to tell a mild-mannered member of the middle class that the classical Greeks saw something inferior in the attachment between man and woman and that what they perceived as more humanly valuable was the homosexual attachment between a teacher and his pupil. Or try to explain to him that until recently a Chinese man would have had many wives, each of whom had a specific role, that he shared his wives with his brothers, that the primary wife was the actual head of the family, and that this structure produced one of the great cultures. What is true of marriage applies to all other traditional social structures as well. The family with which we are acquainted—father, mother, and children—is a late consequence of the industrial revolution, and those of us who come from farm backgrounds know that this abridged family with its absent fathers and ostracized grandparents was considered barbaric until only a few decades ago. As far as the nation is concerned, try to tell a nationalist that the concept of nation was more or less contrived out of whole cloth by seventeenth- and eighteenth-century French intellectuals and that somewhat earlier the word *nation* would at most have conjured up images of student associations at a few old universities. End of digression.

❦ ❦ ❦ All human social structures are inventions, conventions. If there ever was a biologically determined social form—something perhaps like that of the notorious hordes in which sons killed their fathers so they could sleep with their mothers—our sympathies for it would be quite limited. It is abhorrent to try to live "naturally." This is, incidentally, an important argument against all friends of nature, who have been plying their trade since the eighteenth century at the earliest. If such a thing as nature exists at all, whether in our surroundings or in ourselves, the important thing is to dominate and master it. That is what gives dignity to human life. Nonetheless, even if no such natural social form exists, the forms that have been sanctified by tradition function as if second nature. Even though marriage has been cheapened by second-rate fiction and Hollywood, it did until recently continue to function like a gift of nature. Our present way of life, in which many choose to remain unmarried, seems unnatural to the older generation. I'm sure that this remark looks like a return to the digression I just concluded, but my intent is different. What I mean is that even those who are aware of the origins of marriage find that it contains meaning for them. It may well be that some lawgiver or legalist or, more likely, some poet simply invented marriage as a bond of love between two people. Even so, a person who feels this bond, which was at one time called faithfulness, cannot live without it. To give an example that goes back even further, it may well be that the subjection of the student by the master or the responsibility of the master for his student was an unprecedented invention by the organizers of the medieval guilds and universities. But those among us who had the extraordinary good fortune of having had a master or a student know very well how valuable and even irreplaceable such a relationship can be. I say this with the intention of acknowledging what is valuable at the heart of the concept "nation," because in what follows I will inveigh against the nation and a fortiori against nationalism. What I say in the following is meant to prevent our tossing out the baby with the bath water.

To clarify the existential difference between a person's involvement in marriage and in nation, I ask you to recall the implicit definition of heathenism by the Hebrew prophets. They believed that heathenism was a crime, and above all stupid, because those who worshiped idols loved a thing that could not return their love. That is an exact description of nationalism. The nation is an idol. When I commit myself to fidelity to my wife, that is, commit myself to an attachment out of free will, I do so because I recognize in her another human being, one who can love me in return. If I freely commit myself to death to the Fatherland out of hot passion, I am committing a criminal act and I'm a fool. Because no matter what the nation might have been called, and no matter what positive attributes it might harbor at its core, it cannot love me in return. I cannot recognize myself in it. My involvement on its behalf is an existential lie.

I have begun to inveigh against nationalism, and not only for theoretical, or let us say, ontological reasons. Ever since the invention of the nation, since the nation-state did away with dynasties, involvement on behalf of nationalism has time and time again criminally and stupidly bathed Europe and the world in blood. It is absurd enough to give one's life for the kaiser or for some other paternal figure of the realm and take the lives of others in the process. But to do the same in heightened measure in the name of the Catalonian, Basque, or Sorb nation—not to mention horrible monstrosities like the French and German—would beggar the imagination if it hadn't in fact already occurred. Because at least dynasties are human; nations are neuter and sterile.

This is why I, like so many other young people of my generation, viewed the emergence of the council republics as a catharsis, the result of a deadly blindness and infatuation. To say this here and now must sound to younger generations like an admission of complete blindness on my part. We all know about the serial crimes committed in the name or under the cloak of the council republics, not least of all the pact that they made with the uninhibited nationalism of the Nazis. And we all know about their grievous end—grievous not because they collapsed but because they spawned a dragon's brood of national states such as Lithuania and Moldavia, which they had originally been founded to replace and supersede. It is grievous in both senses: worthy of a grievance against it and worthy of grief. I want to express my sense of grief to the younger generations to acknowledge my own blindness but also to make them aware of their own.

Back then, during the lost 1930s, it appeared that the council republics might constitute an instrument of reason against the insanity of nationalism. There people got together in councils to create a meaningful community life, and they organized this commission participation as a ladder. Problems that arose in people's immediate lives, such as in labor groups, schools, factories, or towns, were worked on at the lowest rung. These sent representatives to the next-higher rung, where higher councils considered more wide-ranging problems, and so on, all the way up to the Supreme Soviet, where representatives of councils of the councils of the councils were to solve all humankind's problems, once all humankind had joined the Union of Council Republics. At least in theory, according to this scheme, the Supreme Soviet was an expression of human reason whose structure superseded all previous ideologies, especially nationalism. But the Moscow trials dashed any hope for the victory of reason in the commissar system, and I believe that those who harbored this hope have never recovered from the shock. But at least one aspect of this massive experiment in creating reasonable human structures instead of ideologically loaded ones endured, even after the shock. The previous murderous ideologies, especially nationalism, were smashed by the council republics. And Behold! The council republics collapse, but nationalism, which was thought to be dead for seventy years, arises from the ashes like a phoenix.

⚜ ⚜ ⚜   I look on with anguish at the gleeful wonderment with which Western societies greet this catastrophe. We, the generation that came of age between the wars, were blind. But today's youth is even blinder. Given the recrudescence of national insanity that we have witnessed of late, who can still hope that a more humane way of life will emerge? How, for example, can anyone believe that a new European organization could possibly vanquish nationalism where the council republics failed? Because whatever else a new Europe might be, it will consist in a superficial alliance of nation-states, whereas the council republics aimed at a fundamental restructuring of society. Their goal, after all, was not only to do away with the nation-state but to allow the state itself to wither away.

But the whole matter has an even more terrible side. All the talk of posthistory is predicated on the idea that we are making a transition from a processual to a more formalistic way of thinking and are therefore freeing ourselves from historical, political, and other ideologies. Seen from this perspective, the council republics had a posthistorical quality *avant la lettre*. Their collapse demonstrates how historical consciousness in its worst form—namely, nationalism—can swamp posthistorical consciousness and neutralize it. In short, the demise of the Soviet Union demonstrates just how blind we are if we believe that a programmatic, designing, and planning mentality can overcome murderous mayhem stemming from political ideologies.

These remarks might appear to have left the subject contained in my title—Does the French nation still exist?—completely untouched. Wrong. In fact, that is the only thing that I have been talking about. And here is the answer to the rhetorical question contained therein: Yes. It still exists. Which proves how blinded are those who hope that social structures that have been exposed as criminal and hollow can be superseded by a posthistorical, formalistic, nonemotional, in short, more humane, way of thinking. The French nation, this invention of the French Enlightenment, has fostered the creation of countless other nations. And this has given rise to indescribable horrors all over the world, and this fact has penetrated our consciousness as a result of a multiplicity of analyses. And yet the French nation continues to exist. This is one more reason for humans to despair in our ability to overcome the defects in our own being.

⚘ ⚘ ⚘ Exile and Creativity

It is not the purpose of this essay to examine the existential and religious connotations of the concept of *exile*. But everything that is said here should resonate with what Christians mean when they speak of the exile from paradise, with what Jewish mystics mean when they speak of the exile of the divine spirit from the world, and with what existentialism means when it analyses the condition of man as a foreigner in the world. This should resonate with all that I say here, even though I won't say it explicitly. My intent here will be to view exile as a challenge to creativity.

Here is the hypothesis I propose. The expellee has been torn out of his accustomed surroundings or has torn himself out of them. Custom and habit are a blanket that covers over reality as it exists. In our accustomed surroundings we notice only change, not what remains constant. Only change conveys information to a person who inhabits a dwelling; the permanent fixtures of his life are redundant. But in exile everything is unusual. Exile is an ocean of chaotic information. The lack of redundancy does not allow the exile to receive this information blizzard as meaningful messages. Because exile is extraordinary, it is uninhabitable. To be able to live there, the expellee must first transform the information swirling about him into meaningful messages; that is, he must process the data. This is a matter of life and death. If he is not able to process the data, he will be swamped and consumed by the waves of exile breaking over him. Data processing is synonymous with creation. If he is not to perish, the expellee must be creative.

Before defending my hypothesis, I wish to draw attention to the fact that it advances a positive valuation of expulsion. In a situation in which we have become used to pitying expellees, such a positive valuation is itself unusual and should therefore, according to the hypothesis, be informative per se. Because it appears that, according to this valuation, those who try to "help" expellees to become ordinary again are actually trying to draw them back into their own ordinariness. This is an informative statement because it forces us to reconsider the usual and the ordinary. This statement in no way justifies the expellers but actually demonstrates their vulgarity. Expellees were disturbing factors and were removed to make the surroundings even more ordinary than before. However, the statement does pose the question of whether the expellers might not really have done a service to the expellees, although neither of them intended this outcome.

I specifically speak of "expellees" and not "refugees" or "emigrants" to stress the extent of the problem that I have raised. Because I am talking not just about the phenomenon of boat people, or Palestinians, or the Jewish emigration from Hitler's Europe but also about the expulsion of the older generation from the world of their children and grandchildren and the expulsion of humanists from the world of apparatuses. We are living in a period of expulsion. If we place a positive value on it, then the future will appear less bleak.

This essay was written by an expellee in multiple senses. And having been expelled several times, he knows well the sorrow that each exile brings, as well as the shadow that this sorrow throws. The German language coined the word *Heimweh* to express this sorrow. In spite of his experience, or perhaps because of it, this author will praise the condition of expulsion.

Habit is like a fluffy blanket. It rounds off all corners and damps all noise. It is unaesthetic (from *aisthestai,* "to perceive") because it prevents us from perceiving information such as corners or noises. Habit is felt as pleasant because it screens out perceptions and because it anesthetizes. It is comforting. Habit makes everything nice and quiet. Every environment that we have gotten used to is pretty and nice, and this prettiness is one of the sources of love of Fatherland, which confuses prettiness with beauty. Discovery begins as soon as the blanket is pulled away. Everything is then seen as unusual, monstrous, and "unsettling" in the true sense of the word. To understand this one merely has to consider one's own right hand and finger movements from the point of view of, say, a Martian. It becomes an octopus-like monstrosity. The Greeks called this discovery of the uncovered *a-letheia*, a word that we translate as *truth*.

It is not as if we could actually be expelled by our own right hand, unless, of course, we had it amputated. Rather, the discovery of how monstrous our physical contingence is results from our uncanny ability to expel our bodies in our thoughts. Such radical exile cannot be kept up for long. An irresistible homesickness grabs at our nice bodies, and we reimmigrate. And yet this case of extreme exile is revealing. For the expellee it is almost as if he had been expelled from his own body. As if he had to get out of his own skin. Even the customary things that he takes along give him a sense of unease. Everything around and inside him becomes angular and noisy. He is driven to discovery and truth.

The state of transcendence in which the expellee finds himself (to whatever extent the word *find* is appropriate, because in reality he is lost) causes everything around him and in him to appear provisional and transitory. In habit only changes are perceived. In exile everything is perceived to be undergoing change, and the expellee perceives absolutely everything as a challenge to himself to be changed. In exile, where the blanket of habit has been pulled off, the expellee becomes a revolutionary, even if only to the extent that he is able to live there. Because of this the suspicions that greet the expellee in his New Land are fully justified. His move to the New Land in fact punctures the habitual and threatens its prettiness.

But the New Land is a new land only for the expellee. He will discover America wherever he is driven. It is an old land for the inhabitants who are called on to accept him. Only the immigrant to America is truly an American, and he is an American even if he should immigrate to an ancient land such as Jerusalem. He spreads an American aura about him by his very move into exile. He becomes the epicenter of an earthquake that is experienced as a toppling of the usual course of things by long-established inhabitants. But from his perspective things look virtually the opposite: he tries with all his might to make the unusual (that is, almost everything) livable. This mutual misunderstanding can lead to a creative dialogue between the expellee and the settled inhabitant.

But where one is expelled to is not unimportant. True, the expellee experiences all exile as a New Land. But for the long-settled inhabitant each land has a different character with different habits and customs that conceal the truth. There are countries that consider themselves new out of habit, including America, the land of our grandchildren, and the land of automatic apparatuses. And there are lands that out of habit consider themselves old, that is, *sacred*. These might include Jerusalem, as just mentioned, the land of linear texts, and the land of bourgeois values. Now when the expellee moves to a new such country, he forces the settled inhabitants to discover their senility, crusted over by habit. And if he moves to a country that considers itself sacred, he forces its inhabitants to discover that its sacredness is a habit. On the one hand he forces Americans, grandchildren, and technological functionaries to discover that they themselves are something that has always been. On the other hand the Jerusalemites, writers, and defenders of eternal verities discover that they are sluggish beasts of habit. As a result, the creative dialogue between expellees and long-settled inhabitants is of two types. One type (say, between an expellee and a New Yorker) will lead to an informed renewal; the other type (say, between an expellee and a Jerusalemite) will lead to an informed desacralization. This classification is necessary to understand the present, including the phenomenon of the "guest worker" or the critique of apparatuses, as currently purveyed by the Greens in Germany.*

❦ ❦ ❦   Expellees are uprooted people who try to uproot everything around them so that they may strike roots. And they do this spontaneously, simply because they were expelled. This is the same process that occurs with vegetables, which one may observe when one replants a tree. Occasionally the expellee will become conscious of the vegetable/vegetative aspect of his exile. He may discover that a human being is not a tree. And that human dignity may consist precisely in not having roots. That the human being becomes human only when

*The German "Green" party (Die Grünen) was founded in 1980, concentrating on ecological and social-democratic agendas. As part of a coalition with the SPD (Social-Democratic Party), the Greens were voted into office for a four-year term with Chancellor Gerhard Schröder in 1998.

he hacks off the vegetable roots that tie him down. There is an unflattering word in German: *Luftmensch* [lit., "air person"].* The expellee may discover that air and spirit are closely related concepts and that *Luftmensch* therefore means human pure and simple. Such a discovery represents a dialectical transformation in the relationship between the expellee and the expeller. Before that discovery, the expeller is the active pole; the expellee, the passive. Afterward the expeller becomes the victim and the expellee, the perpetrator. It is the discovery that history is made not by the expellers but by the expellees. The Jews are not a part of Nazi history. To the contrary, the Nazis are part of Jewish history. Our grandparents are not a part of our life story, but our grandchildren are. We are not a part of the history of automatic apparatuses; they are a part of our history. The more radically we are driven into exile by the Nazis, our grandchildren, or apparatuses, the more history we make, the more we transcend. But that is not what is critical about the discovery that we aren't trees, that rootless beings make history. What is critical is the discovery of how hard it is not to strike new roots. Habit is not merely a fluffy blanket that conceals all; it is also a mud bath that is very pleasant to muck about in. Homesickness is *nostalgie de la boue*,† and one can make oneself comfortable anywhere, even in exile. *Ubi bene, ibi patria*.‡ The discovery that we aren't trees demands of the expellee that he continually renew his understanding of the temptations of the mud. To remain expelled means that one continually remains open to expulsion.

Of course, this poses the question of freedom.§ The discovery that rootlessness is the condition of human dignity seems to encroach on the freedom to come and go, to reduce it to a whispering of the spirit. And in fact the question of freedom now turns on the question whether it is possible to desire expulsion. Is there a contradiction be-

---

Luftmensch is actually used in Yiddish to describe a dreamer or an unrealistic person. The closest German term would be *Luftikus*.

†French: literally, "nostalgia for mud"; it refers to a yearning for what is base.

‡Latin: "where things are well, there is the fatherland."

§For a more extensive discussion of freedom, see Vilém Flusser, "Zeichen der Freiheit," in *Zeichen der Freiheit*, ed. Gerhard Johann Lischka (Wabern-Bern: Benteli-Wer Verlag AG, 1992), 44–53.

tween "allowing" and "wanting," and is it even possible to call on fate? An old question. But for the expellee the question is not a theoretical one, a sort of dialectic between determinism and freedom, but rather a practical one. The first expulsion was weathered, and it proved to be productive. And then exile begins to turn into habit. Should one, like Munchhausen, try to yank oneself by one's own hair out of this habit, or should one provoke a new expulsion? Posed this way, the question of freedom is no longer one of coming and going but one of remaining foreign, of remaining different from the others.

⚜ ⚜ ⚜   At the outset I stated that creating is synonymous with data processing. What I meant was that the creation of new information depends on the synthesis of prior information. Such a synthesis consists in an exchange of information and storing this information in individual memory or various memories. One can therefore speak of creation as a dialogic process, in which either an internal or external dialogue takes place. The arrival of expellees in exile evokes external dialogues, and a beehive of creativity spontaneously surrounds the expellee. He becomes the catalyst for the synthesis of new information. If, however, he becomes aware that his dignity resides in his rootlessness, an inner dialogue develops that consists of an exchange between the information that he brought with him and the ocean of waves of information that wash about him in his exile. At this point he attempts to make creative sense of what he brought with him as well as of the chaos that surrounds him in the present. When such internal and external dialogues resonate with each other, not only the world but the settled inhabitants and expellees as well are transformed creatively. That is what I meant when I said that the freedom of the expellee consists in remaining foreign, different from the others. It is the freedom to change oneself and others.

The expellee is the Other of others. That means that he is different from others and that they remain different for him. He himself is the Other of others, and this is the only identity that he can form for himself. And his arrival in exile allows the settled inhabitants to discover that they can create their identity only in relation to him. What develops on his arrival is a cracking open of the "self" and an opening up to others. A togetherness. The dialogic spirit that characterizes exile may not be one of mutual recognition; it is mostly polemical and even murderous. This is because the expellee threatens the singularity of the settled inhabitants, putting it in question by his own foreignness. But even such a polemical dialogue is creative, because it, too, leads to a synthesis of new information. Exile, no matter the form, is the incubator of creativity in the service of the new.

❧ ❧ ❧ Conversation between Vilém Flusser and Patrik Tschudin

PATRIK TSCHUDIN: In most interviews the interviewer introduces his guest by pulling out representative items from his biography. In this case I would like to forgo that approach and ask you directly how you might answer questions about your life history . . .

VILÉM FLUSSER: I would evade the question on two counts. The first is methodological. I have always been bothered by the way people's lives are measured objectively in terms of decades, years, and months. I believe that it is a criterion that is completely unsuited to experience and suffering. There are very intense parts and others when very little happens. If you were to feed it all into a computer, you would get some rather strange-looking curves, and it seems to me that biographies should be written to follow those curves. I read somewhere—and perhaps you can confirm this—that one's life is two-thirds over when one is born, that two-thirds of all the experiences one will have over a lifetime occur in the womb. In old age there is a general decline, so that the final twenty years correspond to the first two. But I think that it is one of the tasks of human beings to fight against this biologically conditioned limitation in life. At least I continue to try to live a full life, with my wife as well, so that if one were to measure the intensity and quantity of our lives, the level at which we live would be quite high. There is, of course, a methodological problem: how does one measure experiences? I throw the problem out for consideration, but I don't have an answer to it.

As to my second evasion of your question, I am convinced that the concept of "I," "self," and "identity" is an ideological one and should be abandoned on logical grounds alone. When I identify something, I do so on the basis of a difference from something else.

In other words, when I identify myself, I do so in relation to someone else. In terms of an existential analysis, one would say that "I" is simply that of which someone else says "you." From a psychoanalytic perspective, an "I" is the tip of an iceberg that is floating in the unconscious, which is itself not individual. From the point of view of neurophysiology, what I term "I" is a computation by the central nervous system, which computes an I-consciousness out of incoming stimuli, whether these arise in the environment or from inside. In short, a biography cannot be about some sort of "I." And it seems to me that anyone who tries to describe his own life history has never lived. Rather, I think that a biography consists of the listing of networks through which a current of experiences was run. If I look back on my own life—which I do not do gladly because I prefer to look ahead—but when I do look back on my life, I don't find any sort of identity. I don't think that there is any relationship between the I who is talking to you now, who is linked to you, and exists at this moment as a function of Patrik Tschudin, and the little brat from Prague. So those are my two excuses, and you may now continue to ask me questions.

PT: You mentioned Prague. You were born in Prague in 1920.

VF: You know, I was in Prague three weeks ago, or was it four? Two things surprised me. First of all, the city really is just as unbelievably magnificent as I remembered it. Memory enchants things and beautifies them, but with Prague this was not the case. The city really possesses an incomparable beauty. I actually shouldn't do this, as I was born there, and we know that it is a bad point of departure for any sort of aesthetic critique, but I have to admit that I know of only one city whose magnificence rivals Prague's, and that is Venice. But even as I say it, I am conscious that Venice is a small city, whereas Prague, in spite of its relatively small population, is an imperial city.

   In any case, I was there. And I recognized everything as I walked the streets. Nothing felt foreign to me, but I couldn't recognize myself. In this sense I have lost the nineteen or twenty years that I spent in Prague, which were very important ones for me and my development. Perhaps it is that there are no longer any Jews or Germans there. But if Prague is cleansed of Jews and Germans—Jews cleansed by the Germans, and the Germans, by who knows who—well, once that was done, all that you are left with is a theatrical set. But even that isn't true, because people received me with extraordinary kindness and took me by the scruff of the neck, and even though I was there for only three days, they brought me to a place called the House of Photography, and there I gave an off-the-cuff lecture in Czech. Czech is my mother tongue as you know. I hadn't spoken it in fifty-one years and hadn't seen a printed page of it. It is said that two different speech-processing functions go on in the brain, the structural and the lexical. The structural is lodged much more deeply than the lexical. What I'm trying to say is that I was speaking grammatically correctly but that I had no vocabulary at my disposal. And suddenly my wife called out, "Careful! You're speaking Portuguese!" During the lecture I had slipped from Czech into Portuguese without being aware of it, probably because Portuguese has come to rest in the same place in my brain where Czech is stored, because Portuguese has now become my mother tongue, so to speak.

Why am I telling you all this? Because I'm talking about biography, and because I want to say that even though I know the city, and even though it feels completely empty and alien to me, people—and this out of a misunderstanding on their part—received me very well and wanted to take me captive. You understand what I mean? I am fully aware that this is a recuperative response and that people want to have someone who was out of the country for many years and has returned in some way. And so it came about that I was invited to give a number of lectures in November on the Masaryk Quay— *nomen est omen.** I was invited by a number of Czech places, but it was paid for by the Goethe Institute, which shows that the Czechs don't have any money.†

*Masarykovo nábřeži, named (post-1989) after Tomáš Garrigue Masaryk (1850–1937), the first president (1918–35) of the first Republic of Czechoslovakia (1918–38). Masarykovo nábřeži 32 is the address of the Goethe-Institut Prague, where Flusser gave his last lectures on November 25 and 26, 1991. Flusser died in a car accident on his way back home. I would like to thank Andreas Ströhl for providing this information [AF].

†Actually, in the spring of 1991, Flusser was invited by the Goethe-Institut Prague because of an article on him that had appeared in the German weekly *Die Zeit.* In Prague he was

PT: You mentioned Portuguese. In 1939 you went from Prague via London, where you spent a year—a very important year for you . . .

VF: That's right, a very important year. I came into contact with Anglo-Saxon culture and have become infected by it. And not only by the greatness of the language. You know, English is probably the greatest triumph of the human spirit. If you would like I can enumerate the arguments in favor of my assertion. Should I do that?

PT: Perhaps later.

VF: Well, all right; you're the czar! First, I was enthused by the language, but I never completely mastered it. I write decently well, but everything I say has a Czech accent. That reminds me of a joke, where in the end someone says, "You know, he can speak twenty languages. But I'm not impressed. I can yid in twenty-five languages myself." Not that I "yid," but I do have a Czech accent that follows me everywhere. The second reason was the *tournure*. I absorbed not only the turn of phrase but also the turn of thought that characterizes Anglo-Saxon thinking, and I try to adapt the clarity, decency, and thoroughness of English to my own style. . . . Then I came into direct contact with English philosophy, Hume, for example. What a pleasure! Even though I already knew that the Germans were hell-bent on building ovens, this was one thing they didn't manage to ruin for me, this pleasure in discovering philosophers such as Hume as well as contemporary ones such as Russell. That is why my year in England was so important.

I wanted to enlist in the Czech army, but I'm blind in one eye—I could still see out of the other at the time—and so they rejected me. I eked out a living by writing jazz lyrics, the words for jazz tunes, and I was paid ten shillings for each song. But they only accepted one out of every twenty songs I wrote, and I could hardly live on ten shillings. Back then ten shillings was half a pound. So my wife and I tried to immigrate to somewhere. Actually, we weren't married at the time. But, of course, our path was closed off everywhere because

practically unknown at the time. I would like to thank Andreas Ströhl for providing this information [AF].

we were Jews. However, the Brazilian consul was corrupt, and he accepted relatively small bribes, and so he gave us a Brazilian visa. That was how we came to immigrate to Brazil, and we stayed there for thirty-two years. For that one should get a medal of valor.

PT: You lived in São Paulo. You studied there. And you became a university lecturer there.

VF: Yes, that's quite right. I even became a full professor, but you may strike that if you wish.

PT: A full professor in philosophy.

VF: In—yes, I can't deny it—in philosophy of communications. I was initially a lecturer in philosophy of science and at the same time on the faculty of philosophy at the Polytechnic College, because I have always been of the opinion that technology is what is human, and that technologists are among humankind's greatest, from the inventors of the stone ax to the inventors of the computer. I have always believed that technologists should speak philosophically and not just talk such nonsense, and so I lectured on the philosophy of science at the Polytechnic. And that was almost a disaster because the great hall at the university was not large enough to accommodate everyone, because the people wanted to know something about philosophy. They came in the thousands, and I was like a lion in a cage. The only thing I could do was to fix my gaze on the legs of one of the pretty female students so that I could at least feel I had some contact with the gray mass I had before me.

I had always conceived of science as a discourse, in other words, a form of communication, and I proceeded from there to communications. It was clear to me that science has a great deal in common with art, and so over time I increasingly strayed over to the arts. That was a sign of age. Decent human beings are interested in mathematics; when they get old, they begin to be interested in art. That was how it was with me as well. That was how I became involved with the Biennale and with such silly things as photography and video, et cetera.

PT: You said that you became interested in communications. In one of your earlier essays I read the following sentence, which seems central in this regard: "If we come to see ourselves as a function of everyone else, responsibility will then necessarily take on the same role that individual freedom had previously." Could you explain what you mean by an "I" as a function of everyone else and everyone else as a function of me?

VF: I would proceed from the problem of freedom. It is not at all clear what people mean when they speak of freedom. Do they mean that in spite of contingence, they are to some degree not contingent? Do they mean that although they live in a random world that is not predictable, they can nonetheless predict some things? Because freedom without intentionality makes little sense. I strongly suspect that the word *freedom* is extraordinarily overrated. It is synonymous with *sin*. What was called sin in the Middle Ages came to be called freedom in the modern era, namely, the possibility of opposing fate. And I am not at all sure that there is much actual content in this demagogic word. On the other hand, a great deal is contained in the word *responsibility*. If I am responsible for another, open myself to him and forget myself in the process, this self-forgetting with another person over some matter, because one doesn't lose oneself *in* the other, and one doesn't speak *with* another person, but with him *about* something. When one enters into a responsible relationship with another person, one loses oneself in the matter at hand, and that is a creative situation. That is what science consists of! Science is a dialogue in which people lose themselves in the matter at hand. Just look at Galileo's dialogues!* Or look at Plato's! At those moments something happens that might perhaps be called freedom, namely, creative engagement. I would give to the word *responsibility* the role that was accorded to *freedom* in the nineteenth century.

PT: Where in your biography—biography in the traditional sense—do you see evidence of the correctness of your thesis that the "I" is a function of "others" and vice versa?

VF: That's a good question. It isn't my thesis, and I will demonstrate that to you from my life history. I was a boy of perhaps seventeen, eighteen, when Buber visited Prague. He had a tremendous effect on me. His great black beard, his stature, and his gaze alone! It was

---

*Galileo Galilei, *Dialogue Concerning the Two Chief World Systems: Ptolemaic and Copernican*, published originally in 1632.

the gaze of a visionary. And he didn't speak about the life of dialogue but about the prejudice against God. He expressed it beauti-
fully. It became clear to me from Buber's lecture just what he meant
by "I and you" and by the life of dialogue. And so I gained insight
into the Jewish-Christian wisdom, according to which the only way
to approach God is through the love of one's neighbor. Thanks to
Buber I also came to understand the Jewish prohibition against
graven images. I don't know whether it shares roots with Islam's in-
junction. Humankind is made in the image of God. When I look into
the face of another person, and I open my own face to his gaze, that
is the only form in which I can know God. If I then make images on
the side, I then obstruct my path to the other, and in so doing to the
completely Other. It became clear to me from these two sides that the
concept of an "I" was not merely an ideological blinder but *the* sin
in the Jewish-Christian sense. The Church might say the sin against
the spirit. There is a poem by Angelus Silesius in his *Cherubinischer
Wandersmann* that expresses wonderfully what I am trying to say in
my clumsy way: "Ich weiß, daß ohne mich Gott nicht ein Nu kann
leben. / Werd ich zunicht, Er muß vor Not den Geist aufgeben."*
Even God exists only when I say "you" to him. And of course, I exist
only insofar as God says "you" to me. It sounds very rabbinical.

   Let's stay a little while longer on the subject of biography. I have
a friend. In saying that, I just made a major statement. And this person is a technologist. But he's no run-of-the-mill technologist, because he not only built some of the largest dams in Brazil, such as
the Tres Marias, which is the largest, but in addition to his involvement in technology, he is also an expert on English romantic poetry, and he is a philosopher of science. We have been very close and
in dialogue with each other since the 1950s. He is perhaps responsible for having thoroughly driven out of me the fashionable disdain
of intellectuals for technology and machines. He showed me that in
machines we see the greatest achievements of the human spirit, that

---

*"I know that without me God cannot live at all. / Should I come to naught, He must of ne-
cessity give up the spirit" (Angelus Silesius [1624–77], *The Cherubinic Wanderer*, published
originally in 1657).

to the question about what was the greatest triumph of the spirit in the eighteenth century, we would have to answer that it was the steam boiler or some other invention of that sort. In any case, shortly after the war—he was a young engineer at the time—he had to solve a problem relating to soil mechanics. So he went to see his teacher, Casanova, a very renowned man who introduced soil mechanics at Harvard. He went to see him and said, "I don't know what to do. Can you help me?" And he replied, "I can't, but look over there in the yard. They're building a cube. When they're finished, all of your problems will be solved." The cube that he pointed out to him was the UNIVAC computer. It was, of course, a towering structure that didn't even have the capacity that a PC of today has, but even so it was the solution to an epistemological problem . . .

We invent things out of necessity. We need something and so we invent it. And then we slowly come to see that we have invented something; that we didn't even understand *what* we were inventing. Discovery comes after the invention. We discover in our inventions.

The situation during the first half of the twentieth century was as follows. A method had been invented for expressing processes in terms of mathematical algorithms, and this powerful method—I'm simplifying here—is called the differential equation. Thanks to differential equations, all processes can be expressed formally. If it is true that knowledge is power, then this method has allowed us to become all-knowing and therefore also all-powerful. Because we can formalize all processes—and back then the world was conceived of as a context of processes—in terms of mathematics. And the moment we have formalized them, we have also mastered them. We are all-powerful . . .

But after we formalize them, we still have to make use of them. Knowledge has to be transformed into power. And in order to do that you have to numerate them, which means that you have to take them from that higher level down to the old one, the lower one, and that takes time. And that means that the knowledge is worthless. The breakdown of reason. You know—but you can't do anything with the knowledge. That was the situation in which Nazism and fascism and all these other things developed. I'm not saying that the Nazis knew what I'm talking about—they were complete idiots—but they were conscious of it at some inner level.

So, what was to be done? One had to calculate quickly. The main project of the entire first half of the twentieth century was to make rapid calculations! You have to imagine: hundreds and hundreds of young engineers sat around and calculated and calculated and calculated, and still didn't get anywhere. What really made the difference was fast calculators. Don't give credence to the tale that would have us believe that computers were invented so we could shoot down German pilots over London. Certainly that was an important moment. Our calculations had to be faster than the pilots' ability to evade flak. We had to be able to aim where the pilots would *be* once they took evasive maneuvers. That was certainly one element, but the real reason was in place since the beginning of the twentieth century, namely, the existence of fast adding machines! And those were computers.

And suddenly people discovered something that they had not even been aware that the computer could do. The computer can reduce processes to numbers. In other words, it can calculate. It can factor problems into little stones—calculi. But it can reverse the process and turn the stones back into lines, surfaces, bodies, and moving bodies. It can compute. We still haven't recovered from the realization that entire worlds can be built up out of little stones—it is such a huge thing, such a huge thing!

You know, I am curious. For example, there are conferences devoted entirely to virtual spaces, cyberspace, and interfaces, and what all this nonsense is called. We haven't even digested the fact that we can do it at all, that we can start with virtually nothing—what is a point except nothing, null-dimensional—and make all things out of nothing. May I tell a joke about it? There are three brands of brassieres: Mussolini, Hitler, and Salvation Army. The Mussolini bra makes something out of nothing. The Hitler bra grips the masses. And the Salvation Army bra uplifts the fallen. This making-something-out-of-nothing is something that the computer can actually do. The computer can construct worlds out of null-dimensional points . . .

PT: What does this capacity of the computer mean for our under-standing of ourselves?

VF: We have already discussed the problem of freedom. It is implicit in modern anthropology that the ability to make choices and deci-sions is one of our highest capacities. I think that all political dis-course since the time of Machiavelli has revolved around the ques-tion of freedom of choice, but in a very strange way, because we have set up what are called indirect democracies in which we vote for somebody, that is, we give our right to decide to someone else. This is very strange. It is actually a renunciation of freedom when we del-egate a representative and tell him, "Please decide for me." I myself have never cast a ballot because I see it as beneath my dignity, and actually dirty, to have someone I hardly know make choices in my name . . .

Until the middle of the twentieth century we thought that peo-ple's ability to make decisions was some sort of pinnacle. After all, human dignity resides in our making of choices. But there are peo-ple who have really cudgeled their brains over such concepts. And among these people—Rupperport,* to name one—there are those who have asked, "Can this be formalized? What does it mean to make a decision?"

And they come to the following conclusion. We receive informa-tion concerning a certain problem. A problem is an object. The word *problem* derives from the Greek word for object. Why do we want to solve the problem? That's really the first question. Because it gets in our way, right? We stumble over them. And where are we head-ing? Toward our deaths. It follows that a problem is something that gets in the way of my dying. That is surely a strange thought. What am I doing? I am receiving information regarding this problem. Please don't ask me what *information* is. I've been thinking about this question for thirty years, and I still can't come up with a decent

*Presumably the transcription of the interview should read "Rappoport" or "Rapoport." According to his widow, Edith Flusser, Flusser is referring to Anatol Rapoport (1911–), an emeritus professor of mathematics and psychology and of peace studies at the University of Toronto who has published prolifically on game theory, among numerous other topics. I would like to thank Edith Flusser for providing this information [AF].

answer. So you receive information regarding this problem. And from among all this information you choose one, and now you have made a choice. Supposedly there is human dignity in that. But if you think about it, you come to the conclusion that you never have all the relevant information and that the fact that you only have access to certain specific information already narrows your freedom of choice.

Second, you realize that when you choose a particular alternative, you can never really know whether you made the right choice because you rejected all other potential choices. Because in order to know, you would have had to have made *all* the choices and then chosen from among them. But that can't be done. You rejected all of them, and so you can never know whether you made the right choice. And third, once you have made one choice, the alternative that was chosen fans out into innumerable new alternatives, from among which you must again choose. And once again you have to amputate all but your single choice. What this means is that once you make a choice, you are faced with the necessity of continual and uninterrupted choice until the day you die, and you will never know whether you chose correctly. Seen in this light, freedom of choice is real torture. So, one should really be able to delegate to machines?! That can be done, by making a decision tree. You draw up a chart of all the various alternatives, which as I already mentioned, branch out continually. Then you feed this decision tree into a computer. The outcome is that you reduce each decision into what are called decidemes. You can reduce all decisions such that all psychic phenomena are capable of reduction. The individual turns out to be just like the atom—divisible. As I'm sure you know, the word *individuum* is the Latin translation of the Greek *atom*. When you analyze decisions, you find elements called decidemes, and machines make decisions differently from humans. The machine runs through all possible alternatives. The nicest example is the chess computer. It considers all possible moves up to—not really very far, say 3 to 4 moves. I can't even see one move ahead. After the computer has tried out all possible moves, it chooses the best alternative, and it does the same thing when the situation fans out again. Machines know no desperation. They don't care in the least whether they play well or not. They simply play.

And then there is another matter: nothing that *can* be mechanized is worthy of being done by human beings! To put it another way, a person becomes human to the extent to which he figures out which of one's functions can be mechanized and then delegates those to machines. What remains, that which cannot be mechanized (for the moment, anyway), is that which becomes human. And the complete person is one who cannot be further mechanized. That is something we can't even imagine.

The computer mechanizes freedom of choice. We no longer have to make decisions; rather, we can input the values that the machine needs to make decisions. The Gulf War has already been prewaged: all decisions regarding the war have already been made by computer. This means that we now have the freedom to feed not only decision trees plus alternatives into the machine but also the value criteria [*Werte*] by which the machine makes those decisions. And how do we agree upon those values? We come back to the question of responsibility, openness, and networking. Then, what is truly human is that we, in cooperation with other competent people and machines displaying artificial intelligence, work out the values that are then fed into computers so that they may make decisions. We have crept out past freedom of choice, if I may express it that way. The computer creates a new anthropology.

PT: I again want to quote from an earlier essay of yours, from "Digital Appearance": "Most people continue to think progressively and educationally. They continue to experience, perceive, and interpret the world as a network of causes and effects, and they are eager to break these causal chains to free us from this necessity. Their consciousness thus continues to be linear, literary and literal. It is only those few people who have left this consciousness behind them, who no longer experience the world as a causal chain but who experience, perceive, and interpret the world as random, who no longer think progressively and educationally, but futurologically and analytically within a system or structurally—they are the ones who produce the models for the majority. For example, they program advertising, films, and political programs according to structural criteria, which those who are being manipulated are unable to account for." This is about the contradiction between formal and historical consciousness. Could you perhaps put it in other words and clarify this contradiction for me?

VT: You know, there are occasions when you read a sentence that someone has written and suddenly your entire worldview is changed. I'm sure you've had this experience as well. I experienced one of these moments of transformation when I read Wittgenstein's *Tractatus*. The opening sentence of the *Tractatus* reads, "The world is everything that is the case." I was tremendously perturbed by this because I am old and because I was educated in processual thinking. I would always have said, "The world is everything that happens." After all, I had digested Hegel and Marx, and naturally, like all boys of my generation, I was a Marxist. And suddenly I read this incredible sentence, "The world is everything that is the case." And naturally I immediately thought of dice. It seems to me that this is completely in the spirit of Wittgenstein . . .

The entire stance is antihistorical, and its import is: "There is a context. This context is aleatory. And this context has a structure that must be analyzed." If you think about it, you suddenly have a different view on things, a structural view, a relational view of threads. There are no more things; they no longer exist, and what you are left with are *Sachverhalte,* cases, as Wittgenstein puts it. Heidegger has a wonderful word for it: *Bewandtnis.** How the relationships turn one toward another. This structural, networked image has long been established in the sciences, but it only much later penetrated into our consciousness, largely as a consequence of ecological thinking. Forget about all the idiotic Greens; think about real ecologists! Portmann from Basel, for example, tells the following story.† A type of wild potato grows in Switzerland. This potato has a very specific and strange violet color. And then there is a but-

Bewandtnis has been translated in numerous ways, including "involvement," "relevance," "functionality," and "appliance."

†Adolf Portmann (1897–1982), Swiss biologist.

terfly that lives somewhere in the Bernese Oberland. And this but-terfly has exactly the same color as that potato. In fact, the butterfly feeds exclusively on this potato. And the potato propagates purely thanks to the butterfly. This means that I can view them both as a single organism, a single case, a single *Bewandtnis*. In this case I can say that the potato is the butterfly's digestive apparatus, the but-terfly is the potato's sexual apparatus, and both have the same color. The difference is that the potato's color is the result of a specific chemical change involving chlorophyll. And the butterfly's color is brought about by tiny plates covering its wings that break the light in such a way as to produce the color violet. In other words, the same shade of violet results from a chemical process in one case and an optical one in the other. What we are dealing with is really a sin-gle organism that has color in common and which has integrated itself into an ecosystem on the basis of this color. But the color is the result of a congruence or confluence of two completely differ-ent processes, one chemical and the other optical. This taught me two things. First, it taught me to look at the world ecologically, as a network. And second, it taught me to have respect for complexity, which is opaque.

Darwin stated that the giraffe has a long neck so that it can eat palm leaves, which grow high up. Then he said that palms grow tall so that they may be eaten by giraffes. And the giraffes defecate under the palms, which nourishes them. The palms grow because of the giraffes, and vice versa. But there is something not quite right here. Perhaps it is there that we need to start to see—and at that point, it seems to me, politics collapses. It is the end of politics. Perhaps you don't yet see it, but it is the end of politics, because to see mutual growth, the mutual growth of palm tree and giraffe. And to what end? None whatsoever. They simply grow! That's how it is. It is an ecosystem, and things behave this way in this ecosystem. This is what Wittgenstein means when he says that the world is everything that is the case. It is the case that giraffes standing under palm trees have long necks. That is the case.

PT: But why is that the end of politics?

VF: Because politics says, "be a dignified palm tree, and in order to preserve my freedom as such, I must make the giraffe shit." That is the basis of politics: "Kindly shit here!" But such an approach makes no sense as soon as I think structurally and in terms of systems.

There is a rightist and a leftist politics. I'll reduce them to the same denominator for you. The rightists say, "Society should be good for people," and the leftists say, "People should be good for society." And over this they wage war. I'm talking about decent people on the right and left. A decent rightist says that a society is a good society only when it is good for the individual. And the leftist says that it is the dignity of human beings to offer something to society, something of value. At the very moment that they take the positions that I have outlined, they have both perpetrated complete and total nonsense. Because there is no such thing as society without people. A society that is good for individuals cannot exist, because *it* doesn't exist! And there are no individuals without society. Therefore, there can be no such thing as a person who is good for society, because *it* doesn't exist. *Individual* and *society* are all abstractions. What does exist is an interpersonal relationship, a networking, an intersubjective field of relations, from which I may extrapolate society or the individual. They are both complete abstractions. As a result there can be neither right nor left! And because of this there can be no politics either! Because when I try to fashion a dignified existence, what I am doing is manipulating the structure of the interpersonal relational field. And I can only do that if I am inside it. What I have then achieved is a postpolitical, or telematic, image, and all political involvement appears to be an illusion from this perspective. That is much too short an answer, but you posed the question that way, and so I answer it in abbreviated form.

It is hard to talk about this with a person who is politically engaged, because he will shoot back that I am viewing society as an ant colony and that I stand above it and am merely interested in which way the ants swarm. That is a correct objection. What can one say? The answer is that, yes, one can view humanity as an ant colony, but without diminishing human dignity. To the contrary, we have underscored human dignity as a being-there of one for the other.

It is very difficult. I recently had a little run-in with a Greek photographer in Israel that was based on this misunderstanding. He said, "Your deification of numbers, your deification of machines, and your deification of computers all amount to reification of and contempt for human beings." What was I supposed to answer? I would have had to get to the bottom of what I have been talking about here. I'd have to talk about Wittgenstein, and then via Wittgenstein about Democritus, and then back to mathematics. I would, for example, have to repeat to him that history-destroying sentence of Wittgenstein's: "It does not make sense to say one plus one is two at two o'clock in the afternoon in Semipalatinsk."* I constantly cite this sentence as is, and I'm fairly sick of it by now. Because in order to make someone understand what is transhistorical and transtopical about this formal thought, one has to dig very deep, but at the very moment that you start to think transgeographically and transhistorically—as you must—at that moment all the arguments put forward by politicians begin to sound as if you were talking to a sorcerer . . .

PT: Yesterday you said that all decent persons must be anarchists.

VF: That's a way of broaching the death of politics. An-archy means un-politics. Every decent person should reject identification with a system, or with one or two systems. Instead he should see his dignity in his ability to work for a time with a variety of systems at different times. You know, if you look upon the "I" as an onion consisting of layers of relationships, and you peel away those relationships, there is nothing left. Each of these layers is then an involvement in a system. I am someone who wears a sweater, but I won't become involved with a sweater; rather, it is merely something I can put on and take off again. That, in my opinion, is anarchy. If I have a school-age child, I get involved in a group supporting elementary education. But as soon as my child gets a little older, I spit on anything that has to do with elementary school. I told you yesterday that

---

*"Es hat keinen Sinn zu sagen, daß eins und eins zwei ist, um zwei Uhr nachmittags in Semipalatinsk." Although Flusser appears to be quoting Wittgenstein's *Tractatus Logico-Philosophicus* (4.1272), the exact quotation and its source are unclear. Wittgenstein's text was originally published as *Logisch-Philosophische Abhandlung* in *Annalen der Naturphilosophie* 14 (1921).

I envision something like a Confucian anarchism, an anarchy built upon competence, in which each group is an assemblage of various types of competence. I always come back to chess because it is so simple. There has to be a chess club where there are people who play chess well. And I go to that chess club whenever I want to play. And if I don't want to play chess, I won't do as did the poet Körner: go and die on the battlefield for chess out of fiery patriotism.* I just won't be interested in chess anymore. You know, I believe that patriotism is the greatest obscenity. And I have just returned from a trip to Israel, and I'm a Jew.

PT: What do you think of what is currently going on in Eastern Europe and the Soviet Union? It seems to me that historical thinking is manifesting itself there in its original form.

VF: True, but in a miserable form. Originally historical thinking was something noble. If you read the pre-Socratics or the prophets, the first representatives of historical thinking, that was a great and noble liberation from magic! But now historical thinking has become completely banal, primarily because of printing and compulsory education. Compulsory education is a terrible thing, and if you wish I'll tell you why I am so against it. In any case, historical consciousness has become banal as a result of these things. And people in Lithuania and Romania and everywhere else are now running around in the name of this banal, vulgar denial of the individual . . .

Communism was an extraordinarily elegant idea. It was actually an anarchic idea. The term "council republic" says it all. That was the conception, to abolish the state and authority. In my opinion the analysis of value that they based themselves on was false, because Marxism proceeds from the position that all value is created by work, whereas it is becoming increasingly clear that value emerges from form. In other words, it isn't the worker but the designer who is the source of value. Although its point of departure was a failure, still, it was nineteenth century and an extraordinarily noble idea for the time. It remains one of the most beautiful dreams that mankind

*Theodor Körner (1791–1813), German poet and dramatist.

has ever dreamed. And then that miserable achievement—what's it called?—*real Socialism* came out of it. Millions of people perished in the most miserable circumstances as a result, and their dignity was continually castrated. Nonetheless, this horrible thing covered over even more horrible things that took place in the nineteenth and twentieth centuries in the East. I won't even talk about what was going on in the West . . .

I read recently that the Ukraine is going to become independent. Apart from the fact that the Ukraine is no longer what it was—I mean the Ukraine was an Orthodox country, and now it has been given Galicia, a Catholic country—quite apart from that, the Ukraine really means something to me! It means Hetman!* It means people like Petlura!† There is a poem—I forget who wrote it—called "Petlura's Hands." He strangled people with his own hands. That was his private sport. And this reactionary fascist-Orthodox, black Ukrainian tendency wells back up as soon as the suppressive cover provided by communism is lifted. What I, and I'm not alone in this, see welling up in the East is the horror of the nineteenth century, the horror of the black czarist reaction, the violent slavophile anti-Semitism of people like Dostoyevsky. The very idea that humanity would be healed by the Orthodox church. I'm very afraid of it. For example, Croatia. Have you thought about what Croatia is all about? Think about Ante Pavelic,‡ who collected the eyes of his enemies. I'm not sure that this fits in with what we've been talking about—the fact that I've said that I am afraid. I don't want to end on a sour note, but we don't have much time left.

*He is probably referring to Hetman Skoropadski, whose government was toppled in November 1918 by the "Directorate" under the Socialist politician Petlura.

†Simon Petlura, Ukranian politician and leader of the Ukranian nationalist movement. He commanded Cossack troops who massacred 50,000 Ukranian Jews during the winter of 1919. Forced out of the Ukraine by the Bolsheviks, he went to Paris, where in 1926 he was shot by the Yiddish poet Shalom Schwarzbard, who hoped to bring Petlura's crimes into the open.

‡Dr. Ante Pavelic (1889–1952) was the founder of the nationalistic Ustasha movement in Croatia. He took control of the country when Croatia declared independence on April 10, 1941. Propped up by the Ustasha, which he turned into an elite troop, he took up the nationalist cause and committed indescribable atrocities, particularly against Orthodox Serbs living in Croatia.

"Fear" is not the emotion that characterizes my writings; *hope* is! I believe that we have reached a technological threshold that will allow us to live differently with each other than was heretofore possible. Don't underestimate technology! We have the technological means to open ourselves to others and to talk to people all over the world in order to give meaning to our lives! I think that for the first time we now have the technical ability to overcome geography and history and to relate to each other based on competence and not what one has received. And I am tremendously enthusiastic about this! I am very enthusiastic! I don't believe in this utopia; I don't think it will be followed through to completion, but that doesn't really matter.

May I tell a story? I have no idea whether it is true. It is the third day of the Bolshevik Revolution, and Lenin is sitting somewhere in Saint Petersburg. Trotsky comes running in and says, "Kronstadt has been taken! We are lost!" Or whatever he said. And Lenin answers, "It doesn't matter! We existed for three days!" That's what I mean. It won't be carried to completion, but we are a generation that sees a vision of a utopia. This utopia may have silly names like "telematic," "genetic manipulation," and "cloning"—all these are tremendous developments—and "drugs." Drugs are really something amazing, don't you think? Have you ever considered that when people crusade against drugs, they do so without realizing that they are going against Buddhism. To get to the point, perhaps nothing will come of it in the end, but we have these horizons. The atmosphere—and here I want to conclude, if that is all right with you—the climate in which we are living is a postcatastrophe climate. The catastrophe occurred during the 1940s and 1950s, and the air has cleared, just like after a storm. And perhaps we are now getting a glimpse, even if it should come to nothing in the end! If you allow, I would like to dedicate this interview to that absurd hope.

Vilém Flusser (1920–91), a German Jewish philosopher, fled Prague in 1940 and made his way to Brazil via London. In 1963 he was appointed chair of philosophy of communication at São Paulo University. He returned to Europe in 1972, settling in France, and wrote books in both German and Portuguese. Four of his works have appeared in English: *The Shape of Things: A Philosophy of Design* (Reaktion, 1999), *Toward a Philosophy of Photography* (Reaktion, 2000), *From Subject to Project: Becoming Human* (Free Association Books, 2001), and *Writings* (University of Minnesota Press, 2002).

Anke K. Finger is an assistant professor of German at the University of Connecticut. Her research areas include German modernism, nationalism, feminism, and culture in language learning. She has published in *Feminist Studies* and *Die Unterrichtspraxis/Teaching German* and on experimental writing. She is working on genre and *Gesamtkunstwerk* for a book project.

Kenneth Kronenberg, a professional translator, is the author-translator of *Lives and Letters of an Immigrant Family* (University of Nebraska Press, 1998).

The University of Illinois Press
is a founding member of the
Association of American University Presses.

———————————————————

University of Illinois Press
1325 South Oak Street
Champaign, IL 61820-6903
www.press.uillinois.edu